LEARNER PERFORMANCE IN DISTANCE EDUCATION

LEARNER PERFORMANCE IN DISTANCE EDUCATION

Anil Kumar

Commonwealth

Learner Performance in Distance Education

Edition : 2027

ISBN 81-7169-549-3

Published by :
COMMONWEALTH PUBLISHERS (P) LTD.
4831/24, Govind Lane,
Ansari Road, Darya Ganj,
New Delhi - 110002
Ph. : 23272541, 23242541
e-mail : commonwealthpublishers2016@gmail.com

Distributed by :
ARJUN PUBLISHING HOUSE
4831/24, Govind Lane,
Ansari Road, Darya Ganj,
New Delhi - 110002
Ph. : 23272541, 23242541
e-mail : arjunbooks2001@gmail.com

Laser Typesetting by :
Dimple Computers
Delhi

Printed at :
Milan Enterprises
Delhi

Dedicated to

My

Parents

Foreword

Education is the key aspect to human resource development. National Policy on Education (1986) rightly pointed out that 'education is a unique investment in 'the present and the future'. In providing education, formal system has its own limitations. The formal system is unable to meet the needs of all learners. Thus open learning system has been initiated in the country in order to augment opportunities for those who have either been dropped out or remained deprived of formal education system. Further, open and distance education system also act as an instrument of democratizing education and to make it a lifelong process.

Unlike conventional system, a heterogeneous group of learners enroll to various open and distance learning institutions. The successful completion of the course/ programme is *inter-alia* depends upon their characteristics. The present book entitled '*Learner Performance in Distance Education*' is a pioneer attempt to look into these aspects.

The book is the outcome of a research study undertaken by Dr. Anil Kumar for his Ph.D. degree. In his research study, he explored the open university distance learners' academic self-concept, study habits and attitude towards distance education in relation to their academic performance. The findings of the study highlight the ways to improve the learner performance. Special mention may be given to the role of learner's academic self-concept in predicting the academic performance.

I can confidently say that the findings of the research work undertaken by Dr. Anil Kumar have really added to the existing body of knowledge in the area of open and distance education. I am sure that, this book will be of immense use for the planners, administrators and to those who are associated with open and distance education in the country.

Prof. Mohd. Miyan
Director
Distance Education Programme-DPEP
Indira Ghandhi National Open University
New Delhi

PREFACE

Distance education has earned the credibility of a viable and an effective alternative channel for imparting education at all levels all over the world and India is no exception to it. However, the academic performance of distance learners is usually looked down on account of its low quality or for some other reasons. It is a matter of curiosity and concern for many to know that it is what that matters in the academic performance of distance learners. The present piece of research work is an attempt in this direction.

In the present piece of research, an attempt has been made to explore and investigate the distance learners' academic self-concept, study habits and attitude towards distance education in relation to academic performance at first degree level. The study takes into account of the background characteristics of first degree distance learners and on the three independent variables, namely, academic self-concept, study habits and attitude towards distance education. The scope of the study extends to the prediction of first degree distance learners' academic performance on the basis of these three independent variables and suggestions to improve the academic performance of first degree distance learners.

The book has been reported in five chapters. The first chapter on introduction deals with the present status of distance education, rationale for the study, statement of the problem, conceptual framework, objectives, hypotheses and the delimitations of the present piece of research.

The second chapter reports some of the relevant researches conducted in India and abroad with a discussion there on. The chapter describes the Indian and abroad studies related to self-concept/academic self-concept and academic performance, followed by the studies related to study habits and academic performance in India and abroad and lastly the studies in distance education conducted in India and abroad.

Chapter third delineates the design of the study wherein the method, sampling, tools, procedure for data collection and techniques used for statistical analysis have been briefly explained.

The analysis and interpretation of data, constituting major part of the study, has been reported in chapter four. This chapter has been organised into six parts. Part one provides the data pertaining to the background characteristics of distance learners. Part two dwells into the nature of first degree level distance learners' academic self-concept, study habits and attitude towards distance education. The significance difference in the mean scores of academic self-concept, study habits and attitude towards distance education for the varying backgrounds of distance learners have been presented in part three. Part four provides the relationship of academic self-concept, study habits and attitude towards distance education with academic performance. An attempt to predict the academic performance of first degree level distance learners has been depicted in part five. Part six highlights suggested ways of enhancing academic performance of first degree level distance learners.

The last and fifth chapter is devoted to derivation of major findings. Educational implications of the findings and suggestions for further research have also been enumerated. A select bibliography and appendix have also been given with a view to providing access to the tools and references.

The present piece of work has been planned and conducted to fill much needed research gap in the area of distance learners' academic performance. Needless to mention that howsoever precise techniques be used, an attempt of this kind may not claim to be final, and, as such, it should be seen in the light of delimitations stated. It is, therefore, hoped that this venture would make a humble contribution to the body of knowledge pertaining to the area of distance learners' academic performance. The investigator would feel amply rewarded if it helps even in preparing a ground for further sophisticated researches in the area of distance education.

I express my deep sense of gratitude to Prof. K.K. Vasishtha and Dr. (Mrs.) S.K. Singh for their scholarly supervision and inspiring guidance in carrying out the research study. I am also thankful to the IGNOU authorities for extending their cooperation in conducting the study. I also wish to express my regards to every one those who have come foreword to help me in conducting the study. Last but not the least, I owe a special debt to my wife, my parents and other members of my family who were a great source of strength and inspiration for successful completion of my study.

Anil Kumar

CONTENTS

Chapter *Pages*

LIST OF TABLES

LIST OF FIGURES

LIST OF ABBREVIATIONS

A	Agree
ADE	Attitude towards Distance Education
AIMA	All India Management Association
AIOU	Allama Iqbal Open University
AIU	Association of Indian Universities
AL	Always
AP	Academic Performance
ASC	Academic Self-Concept
ASCS	Academic Self-Concept Scale
B.A.	Bachelor of Arts
B. Com.	Bachelor of Commerce
BDP	Bachelor's Degree Programme
B. Ed.	Bachelor of Education
BPP	Bachelor's Preparatory Programme
B. Sc.	Bachelor of Science
CABE	Central Advisory Board of Education
CBSC	Central Board of Secondary Education
CE	Continuous Evaluation
CMA	Computer Marked Assignment
C.R.	Critical Ratio
D	Disagree
GPA	Grade Point Average
ICCCE	Institute of Correspondence Course and Continuing Education
IGNOU	Indira Gandhi National Open University
MADE	Master of Arts in Distance Education
M. Ed.	Master of Education
M. Phil.	Master of Philosophy
MS	Mostly

NCERT	:	National Council of Educational Research and Training
NIEPA		National Institute of Educational Planning and Administration
NOS		National Open School
NPE		National Policy on Education
OBC		Other Backward Class
OLF		Open Learning Faculty
OLS		Open Learning System
Ph. D.		Doctor of Philosophy
POA		Programme of Action
PU		Punjab University
SA		Strongly Agree
SC		Scheduled Caste
SD		Strongly Disagree
SD		Standard Deviation
SDQ		Self Description Questionnaire
SES		Socio-Economic Status
SH		Study Habits
SPSS		Statistical Packages for Social Sciences
SQ3R		Survey, Question, Read, Recite and Review
ST		Scheduled Tribe
ST		Sometimes
TEE		Term End Examination
TMA		Tutor Marked Assignment
UGC		University Grants Commission
UK		United Kingdom
UD		Undecided

CHAPTER 1

INTRODUCTION

The Constitution of India provides for equal educational opportunities for all. However, the goals envisaged in terms of overall coverage, equitable distribution and quality of education are still very distant in all stages of education. The disparities among male-female, rural-urban and region to region are especially higher and significant in higher education.

The success rate of the efforts towards overcoming these disparities has rather been low. Consequently we could not achieve anything notable during the past five decades. In view of the fact that the world today is experiencing unprecedented changes spurred by the revolution in the information technology, rapidly increasing international trade, the newly emerging global economy envisages the need for trained manpower through higher and professional education. The Government of India have expressed its commitment to promote education in a planned manner. The task, however, is daunting. Almost half of our population does not enjoy access to even basic education. The situation is really pathetic.

Formal system of education has, in general, two constraints. One is spatial and the other is temporal. Education takes place within the campus and in classrooms and laboratories. It is confined to the earlier period of one's life generally from 6 to 25 years of one's age. To quote Honry "Any one who stops learning is old, whether at twenty or eighty. Anyone who keeps learning stays young" (Honry Ford, 1863-1947). In the era of continuing and life long education a new class of learners has emerged and for them education does not terminate at the end of formal schooling. It is a life long process which covers the entire life-span of an individual. So we need today a system that helps transcend these limits of formal system and satisfy the learners' immediate and long term needs. Distance education provides the answer to such situations. It has a prominent role to play for education of the people with focus on the human resource development.

The policies and practices of the Government try to reflect the present demands and needs of the society. Undoubtedly, the new policy on education provided due emphasis on strengthening the distance and open learning systems in the country. Para 3.11 of the National Policy on Education (NPE) (1986) states that 'Life-long education is a cherished goal of the educational process. This presupposes universal literacy. Opportunities will be provided to the youth, housewives, agricultural and industrial workers and professionals to continue the education of their choice, at the pace suited to them. The future thrust will be in the direction of open and distance learning'.

Prof. G. Ram Reddy had analysed the present state of higher education in India and highlighted the potentialities of distance education. In his words, "During the last 45 years, there has been a phenomenal increase in the number of universities and colleges in the country. Yet only less than 5 per cent of the youth in the relevant age group had access to the facilities of higher education. Any increase in the number of conventional institutions of higher education is not going to meet the requirements of ever increasing student population in the country. The need of the hour is to search for alternatives and one such alternative was the distance mode of education" (Reddy, 1992).

However, Prof. Kulandai Swamy went ahead to say that distance education no longer is a matter of choice but a compulsion of time. There are 11 to 20 per cent students of the age in the tertiary education system in many of the developing countries like Egypt, Mexico, Brazil, etc., while it is only 6 to 7 per cent in India. Among the remaining 94 per cent who are outside the system, there are many who are highly motivated, academically talented, but could not go for higher education due mainly to social, economic and geographic constraints. The distance educaion system, besides other objectives, meets the aspirations of these persons" (Kulandai Swamy, 1994). By establishing various directorates of distance education at the conventional universities and state and national level open universities, distance mode of education has earned its credibility as an effective alternative and parallel system of imparting education to the large number of learners in the country.

The National Policy on Education (NPE) (1986) states that 'In our national perception education is essentially for all'. The Programme of Action (POA) of the NPE (1986) further states that "The open learning system augments opportunities for higher education, ensures access, is cost effective and promotes a relevant, flexible and innovative system of education".

Thus one could very well see that, trusting on the potentialities of distance education, it should become a part of the Government's policy to educate the masses at all levels of education. A look into various developments in the field of distance education provides a clear picture of the present status of distance education in India.

Present Status of Distance Education

The concept of distance education in India developed from the system of correspondence education which was initiated in Indian universities in early 1960. The initiation of study through correspondence course has come into being through the pioneering and prophetic vision of Shri K.L. Shrimali, the then Union Education Minister of India. The Committee headed by Prof. D.S. Kothari strongly recommended opening of correspondence courses in the Indian Universities and the first ever education through correspondence was launched in the Delhi University in July, 1962 with the objective of providing an efficient and less expensive method for pursuing studies at Bachelor's degree level.

Within a year, the course attracted a large number of students. Encouraged by its success, the Education Commission (1964-66) recommended fuller exploitation of correspondence education for a wide range of purposes. Consequently, the University Grants Commission (UGC) formulated guidelines for introducing correspondence courses in Indian universities. Three more institutes of Correspondence studies were established in late 1960s. The 1970s saw the introduction of correspondence education in 21 more universities. During the 1960s, only undergraduate courses were started as an experimental measure whereas the 1970s saw the introduction of Postgraduate and diploma/certificate courses as well. During 1980-86, seven more universities started institutes of correspondence studies or Directorates of distance education. Now India has more than 46 traditional universities imparting instruction at all levels including professional and technical courses through distance education (Arora, 1994).

At the secondary level, correspondence education started in 1965 when the Conference of Boards of

Secondary Education recommended correspondence courses with the objective of improving the academic standards of private students. The Board of Secondary Education, Madhya Pradesh, was the first to start correspondence courses for intermediate students in 1965. The Patrachar Vidyalaya, Delhi started correspondence courses in 1968. The Boards of Secondary Education, Rajasthan, Orissa and Uttar Pradesh are the other institutions which offer correspondence education to students of class X-XII.

Distance education through Open Learning System (OLS) came to stay in India in 1979 when an Open School was established under the CBSE in Delhi to cater to the educational needs of out-of-school students of age 14+ group. The school offers a Bridge Course for those who drop out in classes VI, VII or VIII to enable them to enroll for classes IX-X. In 1989, the school was renamed as the National Open School (NOS) with focus as a resource organisation to open schooling at the National level.

During the same time at the higher education level a few universities like Mysore University, SNDT Women's University, Madurai Kamaraj University, Andhra University and Annamalai University adopted open admission policies by relaxing formal qualifications for entry to undergraduate courses. However, these were at the Directorates of distance education of the conventional universities. Establishment of an Open University at Andhra Pradesh changed the total scenario of the distance education activities in the country.

The first ever Open University in the country was established by the Government of Andhra Pradesn in 1982 to provide "access to higher education to the adult population of the state, for upgrading their functional capacities and improving quality of their life in the context of broader social and political objectives of equalisation of educational opportunities and the emergence of a new concept of life-long education". It did not take much time for the Government of India to realise the immeasurable benefits of open universities in the field of higher education. Thus at the National level the Indira Gandhi National Open University (IGNOU), New Delhi came into being in September, 1985 by an Act of Parliament. According to the IGNOU Act (1985), the university has been given the dual mandate of functioning:

(i) as a university to 'provide opportunities for higher education to a large segment of the population and to promote the educational well being of the community', and

(ii) as an apex body 'to encourage the open university and distance education system in the educational pattern of the country and to co-ordinate and determine the standards in such systems' (IGNOU Act, 1985).

The IGNOU, New Delhi started its academic programmes in 1987. Now the university is offering 58 programmes with 372 courses in 10 areas. As on 1st January, 1995, IGNOU has an admission strength of 91,398 and more than 2.41 lakhs students on its roll (Takwale, 1995).

At the state level, Kota Open University, Rajasthan and Nalanda Open University, Bihar were established in 1987. Yashwantrao Chavan Maharashtra Open University established at Nasik in 1989 and Raja Bhoj University, Madhya Pradesh at Bhopal in 1992. The share of enrolment in the open university/distance education system was 11.5 per cent to the total enrolment in higher education in 1992 and is expected to increase about 16.5 per cent by the end of VIII Plan.

The Central Advisory Board of Education (CABE) in

1992 recommended an open university in each state. Few states have took initiative to establish their open universities (*e.g.*, Gujarat and Karnataka). In the sixth convocation of the Indira Gandhi National Open University, New Delhi, the then Union Minister of Human Resource Development called upon "all states to immediately make functional an open university in their respective states" (University News, 1995).

Thus one can see that education through distance mode has come-up as a viable alternative to the formal education in the recent decade and provides an important means of self fulfilment to the willing learners. However, it is not a smooth sailing for one and all. The achievement of distance learners is usually looked down on account of its low quality or for some other reasons. It is a matter of curiosity and concern for many to know that what it is that matters in distance education. The present piece of research is an attempt in this direction with special focus on learner characteristics.

Rationale for the Study

Distance Education is emerging as a distinct discipline by itself and has drawn attention of educational researchers to probe various aspects of this innovation in foreign countries especially in the countries like U.K., Canada and Australia and also now in various Asian countries including India. This is bound to lead further improvement and investigation of a variety of new communication media which are now easily available.

The system has been established and approved widely not as a matter of choice or as an alternative but as a compulsion of the time. It would always be critically evaluated and supported with organised researches both at the individual and institutional level. Various studies/ researches have been conducted from time to time on different aspects of distance education. Recently Holmberg (1995) viewed that 'considering the relative newness of Open Universities, further research on practically every point is desirable. This includes instructional design, motivated student-tutor interaction, the potentials of modern information and communication technology and organisational-administrative concerns as well as theory building and the testing of possible predictive theories.

An analysis of the researches conducted in India at the doctoral level reveals that majority of them were focused on the distance education in the country as a whole or institution wise or on its economy. Sahoo (1994) reported that 'most of the studies are of exploratory type. They are useful in understanding the status of distance education. Only a few studies focus on facilitating decision making of distance education at Macro and Micro levels...' It is evident from the review of studies that empirical researches highlighting the contribution of learner's characteristics to success in distance learning system have been neglected with a few exceptions such as those conducted by Das (1992), and Renu (1990). Other researchers took it as a component in their study *e.g.*, Anand (1979), Gomathi (1982), Khan (1982), Pillai and Mohan (1983), Sahoo (1985).

The impact of organizational and instructional inputs apart, success in distance learning situations is likely to be predicted to a large extent by the background, characteristics, expectations and competence of the distance learner. Distance learning is basically an individual centered system in which the curriculum, policies, methodology, evaluation system, media and communication—all strive to maximize the individual learner's satisfaction and success. What kind of distance learners enter the system, therefore, happens to be an issue of crucial importance for the success and the effectiveness of the entire system. IGNOU course material for Master of Arts in Distance Education (MADE) programme has observed that "..... Research in the areas of student profiles and attitudes, learning process and achievement become one of the important considerations to judge the effectiveness of distance education" (IGNOU Course Material, 1992). Further, Panda and others expressed that '.... the learner is the axis around which the system revolves; and research and development helps to understand the learner more and makes the revolving smoother' (Panda, *et al.*, 1996).

Research on student outcomes in distance education emphasised the learner characteristics as related to success in distance education. Other than the personal background, the psychological factors like intelligence, abilities, level of motivation study skills, degree of self-confidence and self-direction, educational self-concept, previous experience with distance education, attitude towards distance education, aptitude for learning, etc., are also seen contributing to the success in distance learning (Knowels, 1970, 1978; Baath, 1979; Coldeway, 1982, 1986; Woodley, 1983; Rekkedal, 1983; Gomathi, 1982; Renu, 1990).

A careful scrutiny of the meagre research available in the field of distance education leads one to believe that it is growing field with vast research potential. Surveys of research in education in India vouch for it. It is also clear that the battery of predictors generally used to predict the success in formal system may not be adequately do justice. Dearth of researches in the area of distance education particularly at the first degree level on the one hand and inadequacy of existing research evidence to predict the satisfaction and success of distance learners on the other have served as motivating factors for undertaking the present piece of research so as to fill in the important research gap.

In view of the importance of Learner characteristics in the success of the system, the researcher was inclined to study the learner characteristics by focussing on certain variables like academic self-concept, study habits and attitude towards distance education as predictors of academic performance of first degree level distance learners, and hence the problem.

Problem of the Study

The present investigation has been designed to explore and investigate the academic self concept, study habits and attitude towards distance education of first degree level distance learners in relation to the academic performance. The following variables have therefore been incorporated in the execution of the research.

Variables of the Study

(a) Independent Variables

(i) Learners' Academic Self-Concept

(ii) Learners' Study Habits

(iii) Learners' Attitude towards Distance Education

(b) Dependent Variable

(i) Learners' Academic Performance

(c) Moderator Variables

Learners background variables such as

(i) Sex (Male/Female)

(ii) Age (Below 25/25 and above)

(iii) Marital Status (Married/Unmarried)

(iv) Locale (Urban/Rural)

(v) Social Class (SC ST/Non SC ST)

(vi) Academic Stream (Arts/Commerce)

(vii) Educational Level (+ 2 pass/ Non +2)

(viii) Employment Status (Employed/ Unemployed)

(ix) Experience in Distance Learning (Experienced/No experience)

(x) Discontinuity in Studies (1-2 years/More than 2 years)

Statement of the Problem

The problem selected for the study may be precisely stated as under :

> *'An investigation into the Open University Distance Learners' academic self-concept, study habits, and attitude towards distance education in relation to academic performance at first degree level'.*

Conceptual Framework

The present investigation falls in the area of distance education. Like all other areas it may also have certain peculiar characteristics. Further the terminology which is area specific or otherwise needs to be clarified in order to make the research effort more meaningful and user friendly. It is in this context that certain concepts and terms used are contextually elaborated in the following paragraphs.

Distance Education and Its Significance

Various attempts have been made by a number of authors-notably Dohmen (1977), Holmberg (1977), Keegan (1986),

Moore (1973), Baath (1981), Rumble (1989), Garrison (1989), Kaye (1988), Wedemeyer (1977) to define distance education. On analyzing their definitions, one finds that each emphasizing certain aspects of the system. In fact, their definitions have built on practice and reflect different backgrounds and experience of the researchers concerned. However, Desmond Keegan has made an attempt to synthesise most of the definitions and explained the important characteristics of distance education.

Distance education is a form of education characterised by :

- the quasi-permanent separation of teacher and learner throughout the length of the learning process; this distinguishes it from conventional face-to-face education.
- the influence of an educational organisation both in the planning and preparation of learning materials and in the provision of student support services; this distinguishes it from private study and teach-yourself programmes.
- the use of technical media; print, audio, video or computer, to unite teacher and learners and carry the content of the course.
- the provisions of two-way communication so that the student may benefit from or ever initiate a dialogue; this distinguishes it from other uses of technology in education.
- the quasi-permanent absence of the learning group throughout the length of the learning process so that people are usually taught as individuals and not in groups, with the possibility of occasional meetings for both didactic and socialisation purposes.

In addition, there are two socio-cultural determinants which are both necessary pre-conditions and necessary consequences of distance education.

These are :

— The presence of more industrialised features than in conventional oral education.

— The privatisation of institutional learning (Keegan, 1986).

Keegan's definition has been the subject of widespread discussion, criticism and amendment. Even then, the characteristics enumerated by Keegan are basic to the concept of distance education.

A more or less generally accepted definition of distance education was proposed by Holmberg (1990). "The term distance education covers the various forms of teaching and learning at all levels which are not under the continuous, immediate supervision of tutors present with their students in lecture rooms or on the same premises but which nevertheless benefit from the planning, guidance and tuition (*i.e.*, tutoring, teaching) of the staff of a tutorial organization. Its main characteristics is that it relies on non-contiguous, *i.e.* mediated communication. Distance study denotes the activity of the students, distance teaching that of the tutorial organization."

Distance education and open learning system have encompassed the whole world and India is no exception to it. IGNOU has attained the distinction of being recognized as one of the largest open universities in the Asian Region. Since the present problem deals with the distance learners of IGNOU, a few paragraphs have been devoted to describe the academic programmes of IGNOU with special reference to Bachelor's Degree Programme

(BDP) just with a view to putting things in right perspective.

IGNOU Academic Programmes

The IGNOU offers both short-term and long-term programmes leading to Certificate, Diploma or Degrees covering conventional as well as innovative programmes. The programmes have been developed after assessing the learners need for: Certification, improvement of skills, acquisition of professional qualification, self-enrichment, diversification of knowledge etc.

Instructional System

The IGNOU follows a multi-media approach in instruction. It comprises: Self-instructional printed course material packages, assignments for assessment and feedback, supporting audio-video programmes, face to face interaction with academic counsellors at study centres, practical at designated institutions, project work in some programmes, telecast of video programmes on National Network of Doordarshan, broadcast of audio programmes by selected stations cf All India Radio.

A diagrammatic pattern of the instructional systems adopted in IGNOU is presented in Fig. 1.

Course Preparation

Learning material is specially prepared by teams of experts drawn from different Universities/Institutions all over the country as well as in-house faculty. This material is scrutinised by the content experts, supervised by the instructors/unit designers and edited by the language experts at IGNOU before they are finally sent for printing. Similarly, audio and video cassettes are produced in consultation with the course writers, in-house faculty and producers. This material is previewed and reviewed by the faculty as well as outside media experts and edited or

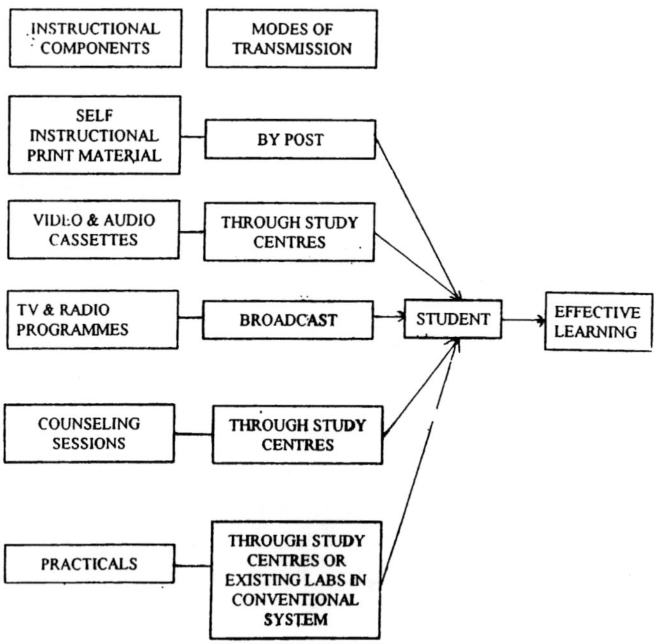

Fig. 1. Instructional System adopted in IGNOU

modified, wherever necessary, before they are finally despatched to the study centres and Doordarshan.

Student Support Services

In order to provide individualised support to its learners, the IGNOU has a large number of Study Centres throughout the country (about 237). These are coordinated by 16 Regional Centres. At the study centres, the students interact with the Academic Counsellors and other students, refer to books in the library, watch or listen to audio and video cassettes and interact with the Coordinator on administrative and academic matters.

Counselling

Academic-counselling is an important learning at IGNOU. Academic counselling includes general counselling and tutoring. General counselling is person-specific, and is related to personal and individual needs. The attempt in general counselling is to make the student decide for himself/herself what is best under the given circumstances, be it a problem of course choice, assignment submission or emotional obstacle. Tutoring is basically course centred and provided by subject specialists or experts. Thus IGNOU's academic counselling consists of informing, advising, counselling and tutoring. Attending counselling session is not compulsory in general. It is for the benefit of the learner to attend the regular academic counselling sessions.

Assignments

Continuous Evaluation (CE) of students progress has been made through assignments. IGNOU uses two types of assignments: Tutor Marked Assignment (TMA) and Computer Marked Assignment (CMA). In some programmes both TMA and CMA are used, and in some only TMAs are used. Grading or marking weightage given to assignments varies from 25 per cent to 50 per cent of the maximum possible score.

Credit System

The IGNOU follows the 'Credit system' for most of its undergraduate programmes. Each credit amounts to 30 hours of study comprising all learning activities. Thus, a four credit course involves 120 hours. This helps the student to understand the academic effort one has to put in, in order to successfully complete a course. Completion of an academic programme requires successful clearing of both the assignments and the term-end examination of each course in a programme.

Evaluation

The IGNOU evaluate the performance of the students through : *(i)* Continuous Evaluation (CE) through assignments, projects work (in some programmes) and, *(ii)* Term End Examination (TEE). The IGNOU conducts TEE twice a year ordinarily in the months of June and December.

IGNOU uses the system of 'Grading' for evaluating students' achievement on five-point scale using letter grade A,B,C,D and E. However, for the undergraduate programmes like BDP, the system of numerical marking is also followed, and the marks secured in assignments, term-end evaluation, etc., are later converted into letter grades. The notional correlates of the letter grades are as follows :

Letter Grade	*Grade Point*	*Range*	*% Level*	*Qualitative Level*
A	5	4.50 & above	Above 70	Excellent
B	4	3.50-4.49	56-70	Very Good
C	3	2.50-3.49	46-55	Good
D	2	1.50-2.49	36-45	Satisfactory
E	1	0-1.49	Upto 35	Unsatisfactory

In each course, a student is required to score at least a letter grade 'D' in each of the components : continuous evaluation and term and examination. However, in the overall computation, he/she must have 'C' grade in each course to claim a degree/diploma. However, in the case of BDP, the minimum overall grade needed is also 'D' only.

Bachelors Degree Programme

The IGNOU offers the Bachelor's Degree Programmes (BDP) learning to B.A., B.Com. and B.Sc. Degree. There are two streams of entry. One is the formal stream to which students who have successfully completed their schooling, that is 10+2 or its equivalent examination, are directly admitted. The other stream is the non-formal stream meant for those who have lesser qualification than that of 10+2 level, but have attained the age of 20 years or more on the date of admission. The latter group will have to undergo Bachelor's Preparatory Programme (BPP) through qualifying the Entrance Test, after that they are admitted to Bachelor's Degree Programme leading to B.A./B.Com. as per their choice. Those who seek admission to B.Sc. Programme must have passed 10+2 or equivalent examination with science subjects. The medium of instruction is both in English and Hindi.

Completion of BDP

For completion of the Bachelor's Degree Programme (BDP) leading to B.A./B.Com./B.Sc., the university allows a minimum period of three years and a maximum of eight years for successful completion of BDP. The IGNOU follows the credit system in organising this programme. Credit weightage is given against each course as below: A student becomes eligible to get a B.A., B.Com./B.Sc. Degree with he/she earns 96 credits as given below :

B.A./B.Com./B.Sc.		*Credits*	
(a)	Foundation Courses	24 Credits	24 Credits
(b)	Elective Courses	64 Credits	56 Credits
(c)	Application	or	
	Oriented Courses	8 Credits	16 Credits
	Total	96 Credits	96 Credits

Research in Distance Education

Research in Distance education is necessary to find out the effectiveness of this educational system and its acceptability for the growing societal needs. It may be in the form of institutional projects or well organised individual projects/studies. As far as the personnel who can conduct such studies in distance education, Calvert suggested that 'the study of distance education is a multi-disciplinary enterprise, researchers with backgrounds in economics, business administration, psychology, sociology, geography and a variety of other disciplines may fruitfully apply their own perspectives to the outstanding questions (Calvert, 1986).

However, a problem that immediately raises in the minds of the academicians when think of research in distance education is that whether or not it has acquired a status of distinct academic discipline. According to Holmberg 'the criteria for a university discipline are usually that there is a body of research encompassing it and that it is taught as a university subject' (Holmberg, 1989). According to Sparkers (1983) 'an academic discipline is an area of academic interest and one that poses sufficient problems to stimulate research and one that leads to the publication of journals in the subject area' (Sparkers, 1983).

In view of various developments taking place around the world, it could be said that distance education has acquired a position of separate discipline by itself through the organised efforts of the educationalists all over the world. Holmberg in (1986) remarked that 'a research discipline of distance education has emerged'. To refer to Panda *et al.*, 'An emerging breed of scholars has been seriously engaged in researching the field and developing literature towards designating the field of study as a discipline by itself' (Panda *et al*; 1996). When we look around the world it is evident that distance education is now being taught by several universities as a separate discipline.

Framework for Distance Education Research

Calvert (1986) given a very useful framework for distance education research by putting many of the elements. The elements are construed as input, process and outcome variables. Input variables are those characteristics of the environment or of the student population that must be taken into account in the design and running of a distance education system. Process variables concern decisions made about development and delivery. Outcome variables are the products of a distance education system that may be used to assess effectiveness and efficiency.

Conceptual Framework for Distance Education Research

Input Variables	*Process Variables*	*Outcome Variables*
Student	Development	Student
Educational background	Curriculum	Enrolment
Perceived needs	Development model	Academic progress
	Design of instruction	
Motivation	Media	Academic performance

	Course workload	
Learning style	Pacing	Use of materials and services
Study environment	Production procedures	Dropout
System	*Delivery*	*System*
National requirements	Recruitment methods	Development
Institutional policy	Academic support	Efficiency
Financial resources	Formal feedback	Cost effectiveness
Human resources		Acceptance in system
Geography		

Terms Defined

Distance Learner: The learners enrolled for a course offered by a Distance Education Institution/University.

Academic Self-Concept : Academic self-concept refers to the experience of one's own being so far as academic concerns are involved. It includes what people come to know about themselves through experience, attention and feedback from others, especially in relation to academic.

Study Habits : Study habits refer to person's method and approach to newer learning. This covers actions taken by the learner with regard to planning, understanding the task, notes taking, concentration, discussion and memorization patterns usually adopted by them.

Attitude towards Distance Education : Attitude shows an evaluative personal reaction in a favourable or unfavourable way to different elements of distance education *viz.*, self-instructional materials, assignment responses, counselling sessions, student support services etc. etc.

Academic Performance : Academic performance refers to the performance of learners in the end of year examination conducted by the institution/university.

First Degree Level : The learners who have taken admission to the course at undergraduate level in different disciplines (like B.A., B.Com. etc.).

Academic Self-Concept and Academic Performance

Self-concept refers to the experience of one's own being. It includes what people come to know about themselves through experience, reflection and feedback from others. Certain researchers in the formal setting have been highlighted the significance of self-concept in prediction of academic performance. Researchers like Shanmuga Sundaram (1983), Singh (1983), Sween (1984) and Pathni (1985) considered self-concept as a factor related to academic achievement of formal students. Singh (1983) found a positive and significant relationship between self-concept and achievement. Pathni (1985) arrived at the conclusion that self-concept is a significant predictor of academic achievement, both actual and perceived. Sween (1984) by using the 'Deo-Personality Word List found that students with high self-concept achieved significantly higher than those with low self-concept. A study conducted by Saraswat (1982) on self-concept, found that among others academic self-concept is more related to academic performance of secondary school students.

In the present context, an effort was made to study a particular dimension of self-concept just to give emphasis to the individual's perception of his/her capabilities to face the academic challenge ahead. Academic self-concept would therefore concern the inner feeling and judgement of the individual to undertake various activities related to the study of various courses without any fear of hesitation thereon. The study, thus makes an attempt to ascertain the relationship of academic self-concept with academic performance of distance learners at first degree level.

Study Habits and Academic Performance

Learning strategies have been found to have considerable impact on achievement. Learning style, learning strategies and individual orientation have been found to be of crucial importance to success in distance education (Coggins, 1988). While summarising a number of studies on the above aspects, Gibbs, Marton and Taylor (1982) explained why students fail to learn through distance education. According to these researchers, this is because *(i)* students lack the necessary study skills; *(ii)* students have limited study approaches; *(iii)* students themselves choose their approaches to study and some choose inappropriate and ineffective approaches, etc.

Further, behavioural patterns of learners as followed in their studies appear to have their impact on their academic achievement. Various researches conducted in the areas of study habits *vis-a-vis* achievement in formal setting have highlighted the importance of various approaches of learners practiced to acquire further knowledge. Study of Rao (1965) underlined the predictive value of study habits for academic achievement. Jain (1964), Kulwant Kaur (1979), Tiwari (1982) and Shanmuga Sundaram (1983) also explored the area further and reported positive and significant association between study habits and scholastic achievement. Singh (1984) observed significant differences in the study habits of boys and girls.

It seems quite reasonable to look into the study habits

of distance learners, who being adults and resuming studies for different motivations, may be practising different patterns of planning for studies, taking notes, memorization and understanding of concepts, working habits, concentration and consultation habits, etc. Accordingly all these variables were studied by using a suitable study habit inventory and relationship were explored for distance learners at first degree level.

Attitude and Academic Performance

Allport (1935) identifies three main features of attitude. They are : *(a)* preparation or readiness for favourable or unfavourable responses, *(b)* which is organised through experience and which activated in the presence of all subjects and situations with which attitude is related. Various researches in the formal setting have tried to show the significance of attitude in prediction of academic performance. Singh (1986) found that high achievers scored high in study attitude while low achievers scored low. Patil (1984) conducted a study on post graduate pupil teachers, showed that their attitude towards teaching and their achievement had a correlation of 0.16 which was found to be positive and significant.

The effectiveness of any distance education programme is believed to be highly dependent upon students' satisfaction with their learning experience (Cookson, 1989). The studies conducted by researchers in correspondence/distance education show that students had shown positive attitude towards the system (Pillai, 1984; Sahoo and Bhat, 1987; Rana, 1986; Panda, 1989).

Needless to mention that the attitude towards distance education may serve as a determinant of academic performance of distance learners. The attitude towards different elements of distance education system like self-instructional materials, assignment responses, counselling sessions, student support service, etc., may influence the academic performance of distance learners. Accordingly attitude towards distance education was included in the battery of predictors for academic performance.

Objectives of the Study

The following objectives have been formulated for the present study :

(i) To assess the background characteristics of the first degree level distance learners of Delhi and adjoining areas.

(ii) To explore the patterns of academic self-concept, study habits and attitudes towards distance education among distance learners of Delhi and adjoining areas.

(iii) To study the significance of differences in the academic self-concepts of first degree level distance learners differing in certain background variables.

(iv) To examine significance of differences in the study habits of first degree level distance learners *vis-a-vis* their background.

(v) To compare the attitude of first degree level distance learners towards distance education in various subgroups based on background variables.

(vi) To study the relationship of academic self-concept with academic performance of distance learners at first degree level.

(vii) To investigate into the association of academic performance with study habits practiced by distance learners at first degree level.

(viii) To examine the extent of dependence between academic performance and attitudes of distance learners towards distance education at first degree level.

(ix) To predict academic performance of first degree level distance learners on the basis of their academic self-concept, study habits and attitude towards distance education.

(x) To study the relative contribution of the predictor variables (Objective ix) towards variance in the criterion *viz.*, academic performance of distance learners at first degree level.

(xi) To draw some significant conclusions with regard to academic performance of first degree level distance learners in the context of the battery of predictor variables.

(xii) To suggest on the basis of findings, various ways of enhancing academic performance of distance learners at first degree level.

Hypotheses of the Study

Hypotheses serve as beacon light in fulfilling the objectives of the study. They form an essential and indispensable part of any study designed to make use of the procedures of inferential statistics for the analysis of its data. The formulation of hypotheses depends partly upon the findings of previous researches and partly on researcher's intuitive, understanding and insight. For the present study, the following hypotheses have been formulated :

(i) First degree level distance learners may be found to vary with regard to academic and socio-economic backgrounds.

(ii) First degree level distance learners may be found

to exhibit varying patterns of academic self-concept, study habits, and attitudes towards distance education as per their background variables.

(iii) First degree level distance learners differ significantly in their academic self-concept according to their varying backgrounds.

(iv) Significant differences exist in the patterns of study habits of first degree level distance learners on the basis of their background variables.

(v) Distance learners at first degree level differ significantly in their attitudes towards distance education with regard to various background variables.

(vi) There exists significant positive relationship between academic self-concept and academic performance of distance learners at first degree level.

(vii) There exists significant positive correlation between study habits and academic performance of distance learners at first degree level.

(viii) Academic performance of first degree level learners is found to show positive and significant correlations with their attitude towards distance education.

(ix) A battery comprising of academic self-concept, study habits and attitude towards Distance Education serves as a good predictor of academic performance of first degree level for the distance learners.

(x) Significant amount of variance in academic performance of distance learners at first degree

level is attributable to the set of predictor variables and high, average and low contributions may be made by study habits, attitude towards distance education and academic self-concept respectively.

Delimitations

The study has been delimited with respect to its area, method, sampling, tools, variables and techniques proposed for the study. However, some of the delimitations are listed below :

(i) The study has been limited only to four variables, namely, Academic Self-concept, Study Habits, Attitude towards Distance Education, and Academic Performance.

(ii) The sample has been limited to 318 Bachelor's Degree Programme (BDP Arts and Commerce stream) distance learners of IGNOU, Regional Centre, Delhi.

(iii) Academic performance of distance learners has been visualized in terms of the marks obtained by them at the term and examination as noted from the marks registers of the Evaluation Division, IGNOU, New Delhi.

(iv) The IGNOU provides a minimum of 3 years and a maximum of 8 years to complete the BDP programme. The Academic performance has been calculated as per the learners' performance at the term end examination held in December, 1994.

(v) A modified version of the study habit inventory developed by S.K. Jain for college students has been used to study the distance learners' study habits.

CHAPTER 2

REVIEW OF RELATED STUDIES

The present chapter aims at giving a brief review of the researches done in the area related to the present investigation. The purpose of reviewing the earlier researches is not only to economise the historical perspective of the present work but also to take cognizance of related studies which have employed one or more variables included in this study. As such these studies have helped the researcher to design his study in avoiding pitfalls. Alternatively, their findings have been utilized to substantiate and support, wherever necessary, the interpretation of the results of the present study. The noted researcher and writer in distance education, Moore (1985), had aptly stated that "I believe the convention of reporting previous research is too neglected today and many of the projects which are reported would have been benefited if more efforts had been put into grounding them in that way".

An intensive survey of the literature related to the present work have been made by the researcher by referring to a large number of journals, books, encyclopedias, International Dissertation Abstracts and national level publications, etc. The researcher came to a conclusion that Indian researches focussing on the learner's characteristics and its relationship with the academic performance of distance learners have been very few. It might be because of the fact that organised research work in distance education started only very recently and many of them look upon the institutional characteristics to give feedback to the institutions. However, quite a few studies which focus on the learner characteristics have been conducted in many foreign countries. Therefore, the researcher tried to collect as much studies which have a relevance with one or the other variables of the present study both in the formal education and the distance education systems. Further, the studies have been reviewed under the following sub-categories:

(i) Studies related to Self-Concept/Academic Self-Concept and Academic Performance in India and abroad.

(ii) Studies related to Study Habits and Academic Performance in India and abroad.

(iii) Studies related to Distance Education in India and abroad.

The studies reported in the sub-categories *(i)* and *(ii)* have mostly been done on the formal education students. Even though the characteristics of distance learners are entirely different from that of formal education students, the attempt here is to report these studies under the assumption that psychological characteristics would not significantly differ much whether the student is in formal or non-formal study setting, but the study should bring out the real picture.

Again in the third sub-category, an intensive attempt has been made to report maximum possible studies/ researches conducted in the area of distance education with special focus on learner characteristics both in India and abroad. The following pages present a brief of such studies.

Studies related to Self-Concept/Academic Self-Concept and Academic Performance

Studies in India

Chisthty (1992) investigated the relationship of achievement motivation, self-concept, personal preferences, students' morale and other ecological correlates in relation to intelligence, socio-economic status and performance of higher secondary tribal students of Rajasthan by collecting data from a sample of IX to XI class tribal students studying in different educational institutions. The results *inter-alia* include that the mean self-concept score was found to be 47 with a SD of 11.64 and with a range 12 to 77. It shows that majority of the tribal students have got poor self-concept and only a few of them have high self-concept. There was a good variation as regards self-concept. Boys and girls differ significantly. Boys mean self-concept was higher than that of the girls. It was found that self-concept also affected the learning behaviour of the children which predict their learning outcomes.

Pathni (1985) studied the psycho-social developmental stage (identity vs role confusion), self-evaluation (self-concept) and need (self-actualizing) as predictors of academic achievement (actual and perceived) by collecting data from a sample of 700 adolescent intermediate college students of Uttar Pradesh. The main findings were: self-concept was a significant predictor of academic achievement actual as well as academic achievement perceived. Self-concept scores shared much of the academic achievement actual scores than perceived scores. No age-wise differences exist in matters of self-concept contributions. However, there exist a gender-wise difference. The contribution of male students' self-concept scores was higher (both academic achievement actual and perceived) than that of female students.

Radha Rani (1983) conducted a study of self-concept and adjustment as factors in academic achievement by studying a sample of 1060 students of class X and XII belonging to different institutions in Uttar Pradesh. The findings *inter-alia* include that self-concept affect academic achievement. The two areas of self-concept which have significant bearing on academic achievement are intellectual and school status and physical appearance and attributes. Self-concept of intellectual and school status has been found to be conducive to high achievement where as the self-concept of physical appearance and attributes has inverse relationship with academic achievement. Difference in academic achievement have been found to influence certain measures of self-concept.

Singh (1983) compared the high and low academic achievers' self-concept by collecting data from a sample of 1524 students studying in class XI of different higher secondary schools in Jabalpur district. The main findings were: a positive and significant relationship was found between self-concept and academic achievement of arts, science and commerce students. In general, there was a comparatively higher relationship between the self-concept and academic achievement of arts students than that of the students studying commerce or science subjects. Again, there was a significant difference in the self-concept of high and low achievers.

Saraswat (1982) conducted a study on self-concept in relation to adjustment, values, academic achievement, socio-economic status and sex of high school students of Delhi by studying a sample of 840 students of class IX from 14 schools under Delhi Administration. The findings were: the boys' self-concept was positively and significantly related to social adjustment, while the girls' self-concept was positively and significantly related to home, health, social, emotional, school as well as total adjustment. The boys' self-concept was positively and significantly related to political and religious values, while the girls' self-concept was not related to any of these values. Only intellectual self-concept was positively and significantly related to academic achievement in both the sex. Boys and girls differed significantly on total self-concept and its physical, social and moral dimensions. Girls were found to be higher on all these dimensions.

Manav (1981) investigated the relationship of attitudes, self-concept and values of professional and non-professional college students with their achievement by taking a sample of 890 students. The findings include that the professional students differed significantly from the non-professional students with regard to attitude towards teachers and society. The non-professional students had more positive attitude towards their teachers and society than the professional students. None of the self-concept variables was found to be significantly related to the students' achievement. There was no relationship between students' attitude and achievement.

Goswami (1978) studied the self-concept of adolescents and its relationship to scholastic achievement and adjustment by studying a sample of class X students from Agra. It was found that the global self-concept of the male adolescents was significantly different from that of the female adolescents. It was found that a positive and significant correlation existed between self-concept and scholastic achievement. This relationship was positive and significant for male-female and rural-urban sub populations. Interestingly the relationship between self-concept and scholastic achievement was stronger among the girls than among the boys.

Rani (1980) studied self-concept and other non-cognitive factors affecting the academic achievement of the scheduled caste (SC) students in the institutions for higher technical education by taking a sample of 60 SC and 60 non-SC undergraduate engineering students from different institutions of Delhi, Bombay, Uttar Pradesh, and Rajasthan. Results indicated a significant relationship of self-concept and academic performance. Only self-concept and reflected self-concept were related significantly to the students' academic achievement. There was a positive and significant relationship between achievement, anxiety and various aspects of self-concept for both SC and the non-SC students.

Hirunval (1980) analyzed pupils' self-concept, academic motivation, classroom climate and academic performance by studying a sample of 1031 central school students of Gujarat. It was concluded that the self-concept and pupils' academic performance were positively related. It also showed that boys scored better on self-concept than girls and urban pupils had better self-concept than rural pupils.

Hom Chaudhuri (1980) studied analytically the correlates of academic performance of college students (Tribal) of Mizoram by surveying the levels of self-concept, anxiety, family influence and socio-economic status and the relationship of these factors and their effect on academic performance. The sample was drawn from 459 pre-university second year students of all the five colleges of Mizoram. The findings *inter-alia* include that self-concept emerged as the most significant correlate of academic performance. There was no significant difference between the girls and boys with regard to self-concept.

Gupta (1978) studied the personality characteristics and academic achievement of scheduled caste and backward class students of the Meerut University by collecting data from students of six colleges of the Meerut

University randomly. The results shows that scheduled caste and backward class students were poor achievers as compared to the non-scheduled caste students. The non-scheduled caste students, the post-graduate as well as graduates presented almost the same order of self-concept as found in the case of the scheduled caste students.

Ram Kumar (1969) studied the relationship between self-concept and achievement in school subjects of prospective university entrants by studying a sample of 2539 college students. The findings were : *(i)* A positive relationship existed between self-concept and achievement (r=0.43), between self-concept and intelligence (r=0.11) and intelligence and achievement (r=0.25), *(ii)* The high and low achievers could be differentiated on their self-concept scores, they could also differentiated when drawn from the sub-samples as boys, girls, urban and rural students, small or big size families and ordinal positions in the family, *(iii)* Low and high achievers classified on residential area, community and family size could be differentiated on self-concept scores, *(iv)* Certain demographic and environmental variables like sex, area of residential community, position in family and educational level of father were related to self-concept, as well as achievement, though the degree varied.

Studies Abroad

Giglotti (1995) investigated the relationship between self-concept of academic ability and academic performance of adult students (28 and older). The data were collected from a large sample of the University of Akron. The results show that self-concept of academic ability is related to academic performance; that certain skill areas predict academic success; and that demographics account for a significant amount of variance in self-concept of academic ability. It was found that self-concept of study and test skills is a good predictor of academic performance. In addition, a student's rank and the number of hours that he/she worked were important predictors of self-concept of academic ability. As the students' rank increased so too did the self-concept of academic skills.

Sylves (1993) explored the relationship between academic achievement and self-concept in adolescents to develop an adequate theoretical model and to develop instruments based on a theoretical model. The premise of the current study was that successful math achievement results in a more positive math self-concept. Overall much information was added to construct self-concept as a result of this experimental study. Support for achievement→ self-concept was provided. The design developed was found to be helpful in describing inter-relationships in the field of self-concept.

Cazenave (1993) studied the effect of self-concept, school atmosphere, motivation, locus of control and attendance on African-American adolescents regarding achievement by collecting data from 146 African-American adolescents. The findings were: the grade, general self-concept, social self-concept, and achievement motivation has significant positive correlations regarding achievement at the 0.001 level of significance. Social self-concept and achievement motivation were the only predictor variables to enter the regression equation at the 0.0004 and 0.0008 levels of significance respectively when a step-wise regression procedure applied.

Marsh, Herbert W. (1993) found the content specificity of relationship between academic achievement and academic self-concept by administering a set of 14 academic self-concept scales related to school performances in eight school subjects for a sample of 507 high school boys. Correlations between matching areas of self-concept and achievement (0.45 to 0.70, mean r=0.57) were much larger than those typically found in previous research. Path models and multi-tract-multi method analysis demonstrated that self-concept/academic achievement relations were very specific to particular school subjects. The findings indicate that components of academic self-concept are more differentiated (*i.e.*, less correlated) than the achievement scores and that relation between academic self-concept and academic achievement is more content specific than has been previously assumed.

Mc Cabe (1992) evaluated the relationship of learning style and academic self-concept to academic achievement and a case study of one gifted school student through a quasi-experimental design with a sample of 93 gifted at one sub-urban high school. The result indicated that academic achievement was high for gifted students who showed a preference for studying in a quiet, warm place, were persistent and parent/teacher motivated, and who preferred to learn in several ways but did not prefer to learn through auditory methods or to move around while studying. This findings were the same regardless of the academic self-concept. The selection of the qualitative portion of the study was based on the relationship among learning style, academic self-concept and low academic achievement. The selected student had a low academic self-concept score, a learning style different from the one stated above and low academic achievement based on the grades during the year in which the testing took place.

Christain (1992) investigated the impact of completion of a basic algebra course on college students' global self-concept and academic self-concept. A pre-test/post-test quasi-experimental and non-equivalent comparison group design was used for the study. The findings indicate that completion of basic algebra course had no significant impact on students' global and academic self-concept when pre-test scores were controlled. These findings, based upon the literature, were expected for global self-concept but were not expected for academic self-concept. The study suggests that programmes, which are specifically designed to develop academic skills, will not automatically produce change in academic self-concept.

House, J. Danel (1992) investigated the relationship between academic self-concept, achievement related expectancies, and college attrition by studying a sample of 996 male and 1328 female college students. The findings show that questionnaire items that assessed students' academic self-concept were better predictors of persistence than were expectancies for success in college. There were some differences between men and women in which variables were significantly associated with persistence. Most notably, self-perceptions of mathematical ability were significantly associated with persistence for both 4 and 8 semesters for women but not for men.

Whlhite, Stephen (1992) studied the self-concept of academic ability, self assessment of memory ability, academic aptitude and study activities as predictors of college course achievement by studying a sample of 196 college students pursuing psychology course. The results indicated that scores in the self-concept of academic ability test, the evaluation of cognitive ability subscales on the study activity survey, the every day memory questionnaire and the concept of mastery test all accounted for significant shares of achievement variance, with self-concept academic ability scores being the best single predictor of students' course achievement. The more positive the students' self-concept of academic ability, the more positive the students' evaluation of cognitive students' self assessment of memory and higher the student scored on the concept mastery test, the better student did in the course.

Eshel, Yohanan and Kuman, Jenny (1992) studied the academic self-concept, accuracy of perceived ability and academic attainment by collecting data from a sample of 192 Israeli elementary school pupils. Regression and path analysis indicated that accuracy of perceived ability has an independent unique effect on academic attainment beyond the effects of academic self-concept and background variables. Different patterns of relation between these variables were found for pupils who tended to overestimate their academic ability and those who were inclined to underestimate it.

Barrg, Christine Therese (1991) examined the relationship among specific domains of self-concept and domains of academic achievement of learning disabled children. The findings include that only one significant correlation ($p<.01$) was found between domains of self-concept and domains of academic achievement. This low correlation existed between reading self-concept and achievement in written language, while investigating the associations among multiple variables such as ability, self-concept domains and achievement domains, a significant relationship between ability and achievement was found; however, above and beyond ability, knowledge of self-concept scores did not add to the relationship with achievement.

Owens, Karen B. (1991) studied an integrative self enhancement and basic skill programme and its impact on students' global self-esteem, academic self-concept and academic performance by studying a sample of 82 college freshman participating in introduction to psychology classes at a two year college. Cross-lagged panel correlation showed academic competence and perceived school satisfaction were causally predominant to academic achievement. The finding support the theoretical proposition that positive self-conceptions are a function of developing competencies. Furthermore, the data suggest that intervention programmes may be more effective by focussing on specific domains of self-concept (Academic self-concept), and integrating self-enhancement and basic skill strategies, both of which centre on developing behavioural and academic competencies needed for scholastic achievement.

Gerald, Steven (1990) studied academic self-concept as a predictor of academic success among freshman university students of 98 minority and low socio economic backgrounds. The findings included that academic self-concept correlated strongly and significantly with grade point average (GPA) while math assessment test scores, reading assessment test scores, and high school average scores did not correlate well with GPA. Analysis showed that academic self-concept was the best predictor of academic success.

Marsh, Harbert W. (1990) studied the causal ordering of academic self-concept and academic achievement through a multiwave, longitudinal panel analysis by collecting data from 1456 students in the grades 10, 11, 12 and one year after graduation. It was found that reported grade averages in grades 11 and 12 were significantly affected by academic self-concept measured the previous year, whereas prior reported grades had no effect on subsequent measures of academic self-concept. The results provide one of the few defensible demonstrations of prior academic self-concept influencing subsequent academic achievement and the appears to be methodologically stronger than previous research.

Pathman, James Keith (1989) compared the self and teacher rating on the academic self-concept of Black and Mexican-American special education students by collecting data from 22 Black and 19 Mexican-American students. The questionnaire (SDQ) was administered on the sample. The findings *inter-alia* include: There was a significant difference found between Blacks and Mexican-American students SDQ reading score. There was a statistically significant difference found between student and teacher ratings on the SDQ reading score. There was a strong relationship found between teachers SDQ reading and student reading achievement. The conclusions were: *(i)* Black student tend to score higher on measures of academic self-concept than Mexican-American students, *(ii)* Black students rate themselves higher than their teachers on measures of academic self-concept and *(iii)* There was a strong relationship between Mexican-American students SDQ math scores and math achievement.

Discussion and Conclusion

The sharp increase in the number of studies on self-concept/academic self-concept is one reflection of the reemphasis on noncongnitive outcomes of education (Shavelson, *et al.*, 1976) Moreover, self-concept is widely valued as a desirable educational goal and is frequently posited as a mediating variable that facilitates the attainment of other desired outcomes such as academic achievement. In fact, the studies reviewed in the previous pages reveal that most of the researchers studied self-concept as one of the many vairables related to academic achievement. However, many studies show a positive and significant relationship between self-concept and academic achievement (Singh, 1983; Goswami, 1978; Saraswat, 1982; Hirunval, 1980; Ram Kumar, 1969; Radha Rani, 1983; Sylves, 1993; Cazenave, 1993; etc.). Further, the positive and significant relationship of academic self-concept with achievement have been explored by researchers like Mc Cabe (1992), and Marsh (1993). The studies of Saraswat (1982) and Radha Rani (1983) revealed that intellectual self-concept was more closely related to academic performance. However, Christain's (1992) study was an exception and reported no significant relationship between academic self-concept and achievement.

Emperical studies showing self-concept as a good predictor of academic performance also reported by many researchers (Pathni, 1990; Chistain, 1992; Giglotti, 1995). Further, the studies of Gerald, Steven (1990), House, J. Danel (1992) and Whlhite, Stephen (1992) revealed academic self-concept as a good predictor of academic success of students at the school level.

An overall conclusion drawn from the above discussion is that number of investigators had tried to find out the relationship between self-concept/academic self-concept and academic peformance. The investigators employed a variety of tools and also used specific research designs for their specific purpose. Moreover, the population and sample have also been different. However, all these studies were carried out on the students of formal system where the education takes place within the four walls of the classroom and confined to the age group below 25 years. Hardly any study has been reported to find out the relationship between academic self-concept and academic performance of distance learners. Hence showing the significance of the present piece of research.

Studies related to Study Habits and Academic Performance

Studies in India

Donga (1993) investigated the factors relating to study skills and reading skills of distance learners by taking a sample of 195 distance learners from IGNOU Regional Centre, Ahmedabad. The findings *inter-alia* revealed that the mean study skills score of male learners was higher than that of female learners. Distance learners with age group upto 30 years had a better study skill scores. Both the study skills and reading skills were equal among the learners coming from the individual and joint families. For graduates and post graduates both the reading skill and study skills were better than the learners with low qualifications.

Raja Mouli and Rao (1993) investigated the study habits of distance learners by drawing a sample of 203 distance learners from Dr. B.R. Ambedkar Open University. The findings include that majority of the open university students had a time schedule. They skipped the graphs and tables while reading a text. They consulted the dictionary when it was needed. Most of the open university students were in the habit of writing and keeping the notes on a subject while a lecture was in progress. Mostly the students of age group of 21-30 years were found following the above methods in order to enhance their study habits.

Omana (1991) investigated the study and problem solving habits of college students by taking a sample of 400 graduate and post-graduate students from different districts of Kerala. The results *inter-alia* revealed that graduate and post-graduate students differed significantly in their study habits. Post-graduates applied better study techniques than graduates. Moreover post-graduates showed a more favourable attitude towards study habits and it was reflected in their study habits and academic achievement. The study again revealed that science students were found to have better habits of study than the arts students and also students having a favourable attitude towards study habits were found to possess better study habits.

Deb, Madhu (1990) investigated the relationship between study habits and achievement of undergraduate home science students by collecting data from a sample of 90 final year B.Sc. Home Science students of colleges of

Home Science. The findings revealed that different components of study habits like home environment and planning of schedule, suggestions and comments, concentration for examination, habits and interests and college environment were positively correlated with the academic performance of students. Another aspect of the study habits *i.e.*, selection of subjects showed non-significant relationship with academic achievement.

Chilimikolland (1987) conducted an action research on study habits and study skills of Metallurgy students of the Government Polytechnic by collecting data randomly from a sample of 51 diploma students for all the 3 year. The important findings were: there existed a moderate positive correlation between study habits and study skills of the three groups of students. The obtained 't' values were below the critical minimum required and as such there were no significant differences in the mean scores of study habits and study skills among the students of three different years. The scores of the students in the study habits inventory were consistent to the maximum for the entire sample together.

Singh (1984) surveyed the study habits of high, middle and low achiever adolescents in relation to their sex, intelligence and socio-economic status by collecting data randomly from a sample of 1600 adolescents students studying IX class in the rural and urban areas of Himachal Pradesh. The results show that adolescent boys had significantly better study habits than adolescent girls. Study habits were related to the academic achievement significantly. High achieving adolescents had significantly better study habits than middle achievers. Middle achievers had significantly better study habits than low achievers. Study habits of adolescent boys and adolescent girls differed significantly at different levels of intelligence, high, middle and low. The triple interaction among academic achievement, intelligence and socio-economic status was not significant in relation to the study habits of either adolescent boys or girls.

Chauhan (1982) investigated the study habits of 10 to 12 years children with regard to their parental profession by taking a sample of 500 children from Hamirpur and Shimla districts of Himachal Pradesh. Parental profession was classified in to 5 types like agriculture, government services (Civil), business, teaching and defence services. The main findings were: *(i)* Urban students possess good study habits than rural students, *(ii)* There was no significant difference in the study habits of boys and girls and *(iii)* The parental profession affects study habits of children.

Tiwari (1982) investigated the study habits and the scholastic performance at three levels of education by studying a sample of 1050 students of classes X, XII and second year degree courses studying in different types of institutions at Varanasi region of Uttar Pradesh. The results indicated that class X students had the highest mean study habits score, significantly different from the students at the other two levels. Students of science scored the highest in all the six measures of the study habits inventory. Girls in all classes and in arts and science courses had better study habits than boys. Urban students had better study habits than rural students. Study habits scores positively and significantly correlated with annual examination marks as well as with pooled teacher ratings. Cluster analysis revealed that attitude to study habits was an important component, while the amount of time for study became a significant factor in the two higher stages.

Saxena (1981) studied self-concept, study habits and school attitude as correlates of socio-economic status (SES) and cultural setting in different divisioners and failures of high school students of Kanpur District by collecting data from a sample of 720 high school and higher secondary students in the age group 13 to 18 years. The findings were: the SES had most significant effect on self-concept, study habits and school attitude of different divisioners as well as failures of high school. The first divisioners belonging to the rural culture had better pattern of study habits than those belonging to the urban cluster. In the case of third divisioners and failures also rural culture significantly promoted study habits than the urban culture. It was interesting to note that the first order interaction setting had no significant effect on self-concept, study habits and school attitude. Also the second order interaction among scholastic achievement, socio-economic status and cultural setting had no significant effect on self-concept, study habits and school attitude.

Sunanda (1980) studied the effect of counselling on the study habits and achievement of women teacher trainees by drawing 13 teacher trainees from three colleges of education for women in Madras. The major findings of the study were: *(i)* The treatment groups that received counselling registered significant gain in their academic performance and study habits scores; *(ii)* The controlled groups had nil or insignificant gain in these two variables; *(iii)* Group centred behavioural counselling was found to be the most effective of the three types of counselling in improving achievement; *(iv)* The personality types had no influence on the academic achievement or study habits.

Shejwal (1980) investigated the study habits of college students by taking a sample of 50 boys and 50 girls of XII and degree classes residing in a hostel exclusively meant for the economically backward students from rural areas. The major findings of the investigation were: *(i)* The mean score for boys was 61.16 and that for girls 56.94. The difference was significant at 0.05 level. The boys were found to have better study habits than the girls. There were sex differences in different aspects of study habits. About 91.0 per cent girls lacked the habits of preparing the topic in advance whereas about 81.0 per cent boys lacked this habit. The habit of notes taking was absent among 50 per cent to 80 per cent students. Learning and memory skills were absent among more than 60 per cent students. The students had problems in planning their time for study, developing good reading habits and taking examinations.

Chhabra (1975) studied certain social psychological variables relating to teachers morale at secondary and college levels by selecting a sample of 410 teachers of intermediate and degree colleges of the Meerut district. The findings *inter-alia* revealed that there was a positive and significant correlation between morale and study habits and morale and adjustment. Positive relationship existed between morale and study habits of post-graduate teachers, whereas the same was absent in the case of trained graduates and teachers with Ph.D. Male and female teachers did not differ in their study habits. Study habits had a positive relationship with educational qualifications. Length of teaching experience did not show significant relationship with study habits.

Trivedi and Patel (1973) compared the performance and study habits of students reading in B.A. (English) and B.A. (non-English) courses of SP University. The findings include that the average performance of students of English stream was better and significant in comparison with the average performance of students of non-English stream; the standard of knowledge of students of non-English group was lower than the average standard of students of English Group. The study habits of students of English stream were relatively better organised than the study habits of non-English stream. Students belonging to English stream had favourable attitude towards English than the students belonging to non-English Stream.

Jain (1967) investigated the relationship between study habits and academic attainment in Uttar Pradesh colleges through a normative data collected from eight universities of Uttar Pradesh. The main findings of the survey were: *(i)* Most of the items included in the study habits inventory discriminated sufficiently between various attainment levels, *(ii)* The scores on the study habits inventory correlated significantly and positively with attainment and the coefficients of correlation ranged from 0.29 for consultation to 0.59 for the working habits.

Rao (1965) conducted a study of some factors related to scholastic achievement by drawing a sample of 500 boys from 12 higher secondary schools of Delhi. The following conclusions drawn from the study about the inter relationships of different variables: *(i)* The three independent variables - intelligence, study habits and school attitude were significantly related to the prediction of scholastic achievement, while socio-economic status was not, *(ii)* The multiple correlation coefficient between achievement score and the scores of intelligence, study habits and attitude towards school was 0.81, which was quite high, *(iii)* The variables, intelligence, study habits and attitude towards school, accounted for 66 per cent of the predictability of the scholastic achievement.

Jamuar (1961) investigated some psychological factors underlying the study habits of college students by taking a sample from college students in Patna. The findings were: *(i)* Study habits were positively related to academic achievement but were not dependent on scholastic aptitude, *(ii)* Though study habits were not related to extroversion-introversion, they were related to the general personality, adjustment as well as home, health social and emotional adjustment, *(iii)* The study habits had a positive relationship with background factors like position in the family, father's occupation, hobbies, future educational and vocational plans of the student and inverse relationship with factors such as age, membership in organisation outside college and sharing household duties, *(iv)* On the other hand, study habits were not related to students interest in reading, music, membership in college societies, sources of recreation, doing some jobs alongwith studies, failure and reward in school, hours of study at home and liking for college, *(v)* Some environmental factors were also related to study habits; lighting had positive relationship but noise and ventilation have negative relationship.

Studies Abroad

Swennumson (1992) studied the effect of the SQ3R study method on reading comprehension of non-traditional college students. It was found that the 't' test of the overall score indicated the non-traditional students made effective use of SQ3R study system, increasing their ability to read paragraphs. Four of the six paragraph categories posted significant 't' test scores indicating an increase in comprehension ability in those areas.

Yeh, Hsiang-Yeng (1991) investigated the relationship of academic achievement to the variables of achievement motivation, study habits, intellectual development and junior college joint entrance examination scores among junior college students in the Republic of China. The results *inter-alia* included that a weak but positive correlation was found between achievement motivation and academic achievement and achievement motivation interacted with study habits when predicting academic achievement. Study habits was the most important predictor on academic achievement, but good students preferred to study hard rather than have better study methods.

Matt, George, *et al.* (1991) examined the influence of high school study habits on achievement in high school and during the first semester of college, using data from 159 female and 93 male freshmen. The same study habits that contributed to success in high school were found to be unrelated to academic achievement during the first semester in college. The findings suggests that college freshmen need to acquire new study habits in order to be academically successful.

Artero (1989) studied the use of measures of study skills and attitudes to predict students' achievement in two types of university courses: *(i)* conforming course, which have high structure, and *(ii)* independent courses, which have low structure by studying a sample of students of five classes in the University of Gaam. The results indicated that the students were found to have weak study skills and attitudes. On the experimental measure, they reported using many of the study techniques considered effective by experts, but they also reported only studying an average of four hours weekly. Students with weaker study skills and prior academic achievement tended to enroll in the independent courses rather than the conforming courses. The SSHA attitude scales predicted independent course grade much better than conforming course grade. The study skills scale of the SSHA predicted grades in both types of course equally well, as did many of the skills measured by the experimental instrument. The test taking measured by this instrument were particularly good predictors of course grade.

Snodgrass (1989) studied the locus of control, achievement motivation and knowledge and use of study skills as factors influencing academic performance in academically talented college students. The results show that the Pearsons product moment correlations indicated significant relationships between study skills and grade point average (GPA). Use of multiple regression showed significance for use of locus of control, achievement motivation, and study skills in combination for the predictor of GPA for the group sampled. Further analysis by regression weights indicated study skills to be the significant variable in the prediction of GPA.

Discussion and Conclusion

Studying has long been the primary mode by which learning take place outside the classroom. One of the widely accepted technique for studying is SQ3R strategy which stands for the initial letters of the five steps in studying a text *i.e.*, Survey, Question, Read, Recall and Review. Swennumson's (1992) study shows an increase in reading comprehension of non-traditional students following SQ3R technique. Many of the studies reviewed in the previous pages reveal that there exists a positive and significant relationship between study habits and academic achievement (Matt, George *et al.* 1991; Deb Madhu, 1990; Singh, 1984; Tiwari, 1982; Saxena, 1981; Jain, 1967; Rao, 1965; Jamuar, 1961). Further, the studies of Rao (1965), Artero (1989) and Yeh (1991) underlined the predictive value of study habits for academic achievement. Raja Mouli and Rao (1993) and Donga (1993) explored the study habits of distance learners.

An analysis of the selected reviews mentioned above indicates positive relationship between study habits and academic achievement of the students in the formal setting. Regarding the study habits, Priyadarshni (1994) pointed out that distance learners have to 'unlearn' the habits learned through the formal school and acquire new learning skills to equip themselves to be self learners. As there is no reported research evidence showing the relationship of distance learners' study habits and achievement, the need to carry out such a study assumes prime significance.

Studies in Distance Education

Studies in India

Srivastava, Manjulika (1995) studied the effectiveness of distance education with special reference to Karnataka state using descriptive survey and documentary method. The sample was drawn from ICCCE, Mysore University and IGNOU Regional Centre, Bangalore. The findings *inter-alia* include that a significant imbalance in the distribution of distance education institutions region/ area-wise and also in the ratio of enrollment in distance education. Regarding the admission procedures adopted, nearly all respondents from ICCCE and 90 per cent of the respondents at IGNOU Regional Centre were satisfied. More than 50 per cent of students from both institutions did not receive the course material on time. All students found the instructional material very useful. A large proportion of students found assignments as a helping tool for term end examination. However, only 11 per cent of respondents received back their evaluated assignments. More than half of the students from ICCCE were satisfied with the present system of examination. But on the contrary more than half of the respondents from IGNOU were not satisfied.

Kaur, Ambika (1995) studied the customer expectation and satisfaction with management courses through distance education offered by the Punjab University (PU), the IGNOU and the All India Management Association (AIMA). The results show that only 9 per cent of the total 429 sampled learners were highly satisfied with the programme. Majority of respondents expressed moderate satisfaction with regard to all study variables like study material, assignments, course utility, administrative backup, etc. However, a chi-square analysis indicated that there was a significant difference among the satisfaction level of respondents studying at IGNOU, AIMA and PU.

Sesharatnam (1994) investigated the Multi Media Instructional System of Dr. B.R. Ambedkar Open University by taking a cross-section of sample from students, academic counsellors and heads of study centres and found that the printed course materials were only partly self-instructional. Further, a significant number of students did not listen to the radio programmes of the university and the increasing potential of video cassette technology had not yet been fully realised by the students of the university.

Reddy (1994) investigated the learners' attitudes and suggestions in distance education by collecting data from 120 distance learners of Dr. B.R. Ambedkar Open University, Hyderabad. The findings are: *(i)* As many as 75 learners reported that the printed materials were interesting and upto their standard, *(ii)* However, learners' perception of course book and non-print media, 50 and 32 learners respectively preferred them. Majority liked the contact classes and reported that they were very much useful for them. About half of the learners had a concern over the time for publication of results.

Vijayalakshmi (1994) studied the role of Distance Education in empowerment of women at Dr. B.R. Ambedkar Open University by selecting a sample of 50 rural and 50 urban women students. The major findings *inter-alia* include that rural students found the printed self-instructional material difficult to comprehend. Half of the rural and urban students did not observe any video lessons at all. Contact-cum-counselling classes were considered useful by most of the respondents.

Singh, Bakhshish (1993) studied the functioning of 4

Open Universities and 29 correspondence course institutes (Distance Education Institutes) as an IGNOU research project 'Distance Education in India: An Indepth Study'. The findings *inter-alia* revealed : *(i)* Maximum concentration of distance learners (66%) was in the southern region and *(ii)* An increase in the female enrolment in correspondence course institutions. *(iii)* Majority of the institutions used only printed lessons for imparting instruction. *(iv)* Study centres were not properly organised and offer very little facilities to the learners. On the basis of the findings he made several recommendations for the proper development of distance teaching institutions.

Das (1992) studied the approaches to learning and academic performance of students in traditional and open universities by taking samples from the IGNOU and two traditional universities students who were undergoing the diploma in Management course. The findings includes that students in Open University significantly differ from students in traditional university in terms of learner, content and context characteristics. Learner, content and context characteristics significantly correlate with approaches to learning and academic performance of students both in open and traditional universities. Academic performance which significantly correlates with approaches to learning could reliably be predicted by using learner, content, context characteristics and approaches to learning of students both in open and traditional universities as predictors.

Mishra (1991) studied the management patterns, costs and academic effectiveness of Distance Education in Indian universities by a purposive multi-phased sampling techniques from certain directorates of correspondence courses. The findings related to the academic effectiveness of distance education showed that the quantitative performance of distance education was comparatively lower than that of the formal education and less satisfying. Moreover, the percentage of students securing first divisions, out of the total pass students, ranged from zero to 2.78 per cent and the third divisioners were maximum in distance education. However, a comparative picture of distance education and private system revealed that the performance of learners in distance education was better than that of the private system.

Jain, Pushpa Devi (1991) conducted an indepth study of the functioning of the Andhra Pradesh Open University by taking a sample of 500 students from the twin cities of Hyderabad and Secunderabad and also from Counsellors and Co-ordinators, etc. The major findings include: *(i)* Most of the respondents felt that the university is not satisfactorily functioning, *(ii)* Study centres were not very useful in solving the problems of students, *(iii)* Course materials were not delivered to students in time, *(iv)* Audio-visual and library services were poor. The quantum of counselling to students was not sufficient.

Rathore (1991) has made a critical evaluation of the systems adopted for the management of teaching and learning in the existing correspondence institutes in India. The findings *inter-alia* revealed: *(i)* The course materials were stereotyped and the institutes failed to exploit the two-way communication through assignments, *(ii)* Most of the institutes have no study centres. Those institutes that have one to five study centres are situated in cities. Rural area students are deprived of the study centre facilities. *(iii)* Continuous evaluation is done in 50 per cent institutions after the completion of course unit.

Venkataiah (1989) suggested a course team approach for the preparation of course materials for distance education. The major findings are : *(i)* Adequate attention must be paid to the writing of course materials, *(ii)* The course team approach of the British Open University, through a very expensive way of writing a course, is feasible, economically viable and justified if the course material is used for a large number of students. In view of large number of students for its courses, this course team approach will be feasible, economically viable and will also ensures good quality of the materials.

Bhattacharya (1991) analysed the scope and possibilities of Open University in relations to the educational thoughts of Tagore and developed a conceptual framework of open university in India by going through the literature. The findings *inter-alia* include that Tagore, the founder of the Visva-Bharati, wanted to shoulder the responsibility of bringing education to people through Sriniketan, the agency for rural extension work. Thus at a time when nobody in the world could even dream of relating university to community through educational programmes, Tagore developed a full-fledged extension programme of the Visva-Bharati through Sriniketan. Distance education programme, known as Laka Siksha Sansad was another striking programme of Sriniketan. Visva Bharati Lakasiksha Sansad removed the space-time barrier of the traditional system for its clientele. It introduced open book system, partial clearance examination, new kind of norms for question paper setting and grading system, etc. There are three functional dimensions of Open University and their nature relevant to the needs of the Indian people. These are : *(i)* Open University as a parallel system, *(ii)* Open University as a supplementary system, *(iii)* Open University as a complementary system.

Pugazhenthi (1991) studied the teacher education programme through correspondence system in the Madurai Kamaraj University by taking a sample of all the

B.Ed. and the M.Ed. students of the academic year 1985-86 along with sample of some teachers, resource persons and guiding teachers. The results indicates that the age of the teacher trainees ranged from 25 to 61 years. About half of the B.Ed. students belonged to the rural areas. The rate of dropouts was below 10 per cent. Physical facilities provided and methodology adopted during contact programmes were not found satisfactory. Most of the students found that the functioning of the study centres inadequate and inefficient. The trainees found it difficult to find a place for practice teaching as well as suitable guiding teachers.

Renu (1990) studied the success in distance learning system in relation to some key learned and institutional variables and found that both learner variables and institutional variables contribute positively to success of distance learning at the B.Ed. Success in distance learning system has been found to be intimately associated with course material, two-way interaction between tutor/ organization and learner personal contact programme, assignment system and system of evaluation. The learners enrolled in B.Ed. through correspondence programme have been found to give a good account of themselves in university examination in theory paper. Contrary to popular belief, distance education has been found almost as effective as full time studies in colleges of education as far as mastery of theoretical knowledge is concerned, as assessed at the end of university examination.

Upretti (1988) studied the impact of teacher learning through correspondence course on upward occupational mobility of the elementary teachers in the Western Region by selecting a sample of 172 elementary teachers. The results indicates that the factors like work place of teachers (home, state or outside), rural-urban background, location of schools, family structure, age, sex, religion and caste of the teachers have affected the vertical mobility from elementary to the secondary level. The inter generational mobility, rural-urban background, the type of management, sex, caste, age and the proximity of home from the place of work, all have influenced the vertical mobility. Teachers from urban background and working in urban schools have more vertical mobility.

Mulay, *et al.* (1986) conducted a study of correspondence education in India by studying 23 institutes of correspondence courses at the university stage along with 63 teachers, 272 students from some of these institutions. The findings *inter-alia* include that some institutions tried some kind of innovative practices in the fields of students' support services, organization of student records and training of academic staff. A high (70) percentage of students was satisfied with the content coverage of lesson scripts. Most of the students expressed satisfaction with regard to personal contact programme activities. They had complained about poor library facilities. The radio programmes were listened to by only 31 per cent of students.

Indradevi (1985) made a philosophical analysis of the concept of distance education and its implications on the emerging non-formal systems of education with special reference to teacher education programmes by taking a sample of 540 distance learners perusing B.Ed. and M.Ed. courses in the Faculty of Education of the Osmania University. The study revealed that the factors which motivated the learners to take up distance mode was the flexible nature of the course, not being able to afford study in the regular course both in terms of money and time and being a woman member of the community. There was no significant relation between respondents' caste and their reactions to the course. The reactions of the correspondents further revealed that distance education suited to middle aged groups and female subjects.

Sahoo (1985) studied the correspondence education in an Indian University by collecting data from the H.P. University through official records and from teachers, students and administrators attached with the correspondence division. His findings *inter-alia* include that the academic and economic factors mostly motivated students to join their studies whereas instructional factors, management factors, utilitarian factors and personal factors come in the way of completion of courses. The correspondence students had poorer performance in the examinations in comparison to that of regular students. However, a selected number of correspondence students performed well at the university level. The utility of correspondence courses was realised by the pass students in terms of academic and sociological aspects but a large chunk of students did not perceive the utility in terms of job placement and occupational growth.

Pillai and Mohan (1984) studied the impact and performance of correspondence education programme of Madurai Kamaraj University by selecting a sample of 3000 candidates randomly from the students who had successfully completed correspondence education. The findings include that the participants were men and majority comes from middle income group and were below 30 years. About 200 convicts in the central prisons of Tamil Nadu also took advantage of correspondence education. Almost all the correspondence courses students found printed lessons most important. Only one third of the candidates felt that contact classes were most useful. Assignments, response sheets and study centres were considered least useful by more than fifty per cent of the students. Radio programmes were, however, considered as most useful or useful by about 68 per cent students.

Ram (1984) evaluated the correspondence education

in terms of cost and academic performance and also to know the attitude of females towards correspondence education by using purposive sampling. The findings *inter-alia* revealed that the academic performance of correspondence education was not higher than the academic performance of regular education both in quantity and quality. The academic performance of correspondence education was better than the academic performance of private education both in quantity and quality. Students and teachers of correspondence education had a favourable attitude toward correspondence education. The attitude of teachers was more favourable than that of students but the difference was not significant. The male and employed students had a favourable attitude while the female and unemployed students had an unfavourable attitude towards correspondence education.

Pillai and Mohan (1983) studied the impact of correspondence education on society by collecting data from 3000 students who had successfully completed correspondence course and those who were undergoing and also from 400 regular students and 50 representatives of public. The findings *inter-alia* include that according to those who had undergone correspondence education maximum impact was in the category of social well being. They said that it had been possible to improve their status and they had utilized their leisure time with advantage. The next impact was in the category of educational well being. The participants reported that they were able to improve their qualifications and had opportunities to learn more in their respective fields of interest. The other benefits reported include better job opportunities, career promotions, financial benefits, ability to write better. The general opinion about correspondence education was that it did give a second chance to people who are missed higher education.

Gomathi (1982) conducted a critical study of the participants evaluation of selected postgraduate course of correspondence education programme of the Madurai Kamaraj University. The findings of the study revealed that there was no significant relationship between the achievement of the candidates and their evaluation regarding the realization of objectives and factors such as lesson units, response sheets, text books, contact seminar, study centres and evaluation. Achievement was associated with the evaluation of radio broadcast and instruction. There were more men (61%) than women candidates (39%). Sixty five per cent of the candidates were employed, of which 45 per cent were teachers.

Khan (1982) studied the suitability of teaching through correspondence courses as offered by some Indian Universities at the first degree level by studying a sample of 43 English teachers working in the correspondence institutions and 100 undergraduate students. The findings include that the majority of the distance learners were teenagers, men and unemployed. Most of the students joined the correspondence courses because of their desire for improvement of qualifications. A large number of students complained about the lack of library facilities, lack of adequate contacts between the tutors and students, and not getting proper instruction through lesson scripts. Majority of them did not submit the assignments and did not consider the personal contact programmes as necessary elements of their studies. As a whole, a large number of students were in favour of correspondence courses, while 34 per cent or them disliked the system.

Biswal (1979) conducted a study on correspondence education in India by collecting data from all the directorates of correspondence education existing in seventies and the Punjabi University and the Madurai

Kamaraj University were selected for studying the academic achievement. The findings *inter-alia* included that there was no significant difference in the academic achievement of the students of formal system and correspondence system. The academic motivation of the students of correspondence education was found to be below normal. Most of the students of correspondence education hailed from the second category of SES. The heads of departments of the directorates of correspondence education felt that suitable teachers were not available to them for development of instructional material. The teachers of correspondence education felt that the workload was more due to which justice to work was not possible.

Saini (1979) investigated the distance teaching prospects and problems. The data were collected by using systematic sampling method from the farmers who were enrolled for one year certificate course in agriculture. The findings include that young respondents with middle and secondary level education comprising potential group for correspondence course. Prior to registration, the farmers knowledge in different aspects of agriculture technology was inadequate which was made up through distance teaching. Majority of the farmers could, reasonably, comprehend the content which they read themselves during their free time. The lessons were effective in imparting information as well as in improving field practices.

Studies Abroad

Riddle (1995) studied the factors which contribute to grade achievement and course satisfaction of distance education system by collecting data from the undergraduate students enrolled in distance education classes in the Education Network of Maine and the North Dokota Interactive Video Network. The results on multiple regression analysis showed that the two variables, namely, full or part-time students status, self efficiency and distance students distance from the originating campus accounted for 20 per cent of the total variance in satisfaction that was predictable. The results further show that the state and field dependence accounted for 45 per cent of the variance in grade that was predictable. Among the significant correlation results was 'the relationship between self-efficacy and locus of control.

Powley (1995) studied the effectiveness of electronic and telecommunications tutoring on distance education students' completion rates, learning outcomes, time to complete, their motivation to participate in future distance education programmes through an experimental design. The results revealed that regularly scheduled tutorial assistance made a significant difference in distance students' course completion rates and motivation towards distance education, but no significant difference was found in students learning or the amount of time to complete the study across the 3 groups. The study concluded that scheduled distance tutoring interventions had some postitive effect on distance students, but distance educators must carefully weigh the costs of establishing the tutor intervention programme.

A case study method was employed by Iskandar (1995) to find-out the efficiency of different methods of providng feedback to distance learners in a developing country Universitas Terbuka (UT), Indonesia. Four methods of feedback were given to the participants enrolled in a differential mathematics course and their effectiveness and efficiency were compared with the criteria like student's satisfaction, adequacy, appropriateness, participation rate, turn-around time of feedback, tutor satisfaction, tutor's time and overall costs. The results show that the students perceived the assignment as an opportunity to open two-way communication with the tutor and to improve their learning strategies. The tutor's direct comments were more effective but required more resources than the pre-produced feedback. The spoken feedback was as effective as the written one.

Li-Chun (1995) investigated the effects of effort and worry on distance learning in the National Open University (NOU) of Taiwan. The data were collected from 598 students who were enrolled in the course 'Selected English Readings' from NOU. The results show that students' state worry, not trait worry had a strong negative influence on their academic achievement. Students' effort investment had no influence on their academic achievement. Students' trait worry had a positive influence on their state worry and on their invested effort in print.

Student satisfaction with distance education at the University of South Carolina as it correlates to medium of instruction, educational level, gender, working status and reasons for enrolment were studied by Price (1994) by collecting data from 2942 students enrolled in the university and taught via instructional television. The results show that there was a correlation between level of students satisfaction with the distance education experience and medium of instruction. It also determined that there was a relation between students satisfaction and the student's level of previous education. There was no correlation between students' satisfaction and gender. There was, however, a correlation between students satisfaction and whether a student was employed.

Sang (1994) investigated the learning strategies and attitudes of adults in a distance basic education programme in Thailand and their relationship to the students' academic achievement (grade point average). The results show that adult learners had much difficulty with test taking strategies, test anxiety, fear and finding time to study. However, their ability to concentrate while studying was high. Most students preferred learning in the group meetings rather than by studying textbooks. Further, the results on learning strategies suggest that for Thai females, self-confidence and self-image are more important to academic success than learning strategies. Further, the result revealed better learning strategies and attitudes for students who relied on textbooks than for students who relied on group meetings to learn the course contents.

Clark (1994) surveyed the faculty attitudes toward college credit distance education in U.S. Public Higher Education. The respondents reported slightly positive attitude towards video conferencing and telecourse study, slightly negative attitude toward computer conferencing and audiographics and moderately negative attitudes towards correspondence study and audio conferencing when used in the delivery of Distance Education. Content analysis of answers to open-ended questions revealed concern about interaction in distance education and other indicators of quality, as well as qualified support for expanded access to higher education via distance education.

Ekins, Judith, M. (1993) investigated skills and approaches to study in distance learning by collecting data from a sample of 549 students from Hongkong/Macau enrolled in under-graduate distance learning courses with East Asian Open Institute. Students rated their study skills on a five point scale. The study skills, upon which students rated themselves highest, were understanding concepts and theories, tackling assignments and reading effectively. Students who had persisted in the system longer rated themselves more highly on some study skills. Students who had gained more credits rated themselves more highly on most study skills. The conclusion was that deep motivation was a key to success, but to succeed in gaining credit and good grades, deep strategy, achieving motive and achieving strategy were also needed.

Saga, Hiroo (1993) conducted a study to find out why and how students of Allama Iqbal Open University (AIOU) in Pakistan learn through its distance education system by collecting data from a sample of 661 B.A. students and 188 tutors. The findings indicated that about 25 per cent of the students were female in age range between 18 to 59 years with an average of 30. The motive behind doing the course was want to make up for lack of studies in the past and love for study. The students were generally confident of success at AIOU and perceived that they had achieved their course work satisfactorily. Students evaluated textbooks and assignments as very effective. However, the tutors perceived reading textbooks, doing assignments and meeting the tutors as the most important elements of studying for students at AIOU. Many of them perceived that AIOU students motivation was higher than that of other regular college students.

Smith, Dennie (1993) compared the graduate students' attitude and academic performance in distance education (off campus students) with an on campus students. The results indicted that final grade score were significantly lower for the host distance class than for the control class taught conventionally. 20 per cent members of the remote class stated a negative opinion about the technology and 32 per cent in the host class reported negative feeling about the course. The technology was very distracting to students in the beginning of the course. However, by the end of the course, most of the students were receptive to distance education as part of the future of instructional delivery, but they still favoured the conventional way of learning. Achievement data were not very conclusive, but the lower grade of the host distance class may reflect their more negative attitudes.

Jegede, *et al.* (1992) studied the students anxiety in learning through distance education by collecting data from 222 students of the University of Southern Queensland enrolled in distance education. The findings reveal that: students exhibited a high anxiety level and were generally more anxious about their studies after the semester than before it. Gender, age, marital status and course of study were not significantly related to students' anxiety in learning through distance education. However, a significant increase was noticed for the factor of time between the students' pre-semester and post-semester opinions, while some increase was noted *inter-alia* for the factors of employment and family support. It may be that while the students found ways to cope with the factors associated with content environment, and readiness, the fact of time, employment, and family support were likely to be associated with more problems than the students had expected.

Hotrabhuvananada, Benjaporn (1992) conducted a study to determine the motivational reaction toward self-instructional materials of Thai Open University by collecting data from 969 respondents purposively from those who used self instructional text only and those who used the text in conjunction with other instructional materials. Findings revealed that the students who used multi-media self-instructional materials in self-study were more likely to be motivated in a self-study course than students who used the text only. Students who had prior experience with self-study are more likely to be motivated in a self-study course than students who have no prior experience.

Grudnoski, Anthong Thomas (1992) studied the attitudes and behaviour toward professional continuing education by distance education means within the professional groups of engineers, lawyers, physicians, teachers and professors by collecting data of 100 respondents with strâtified random sampling method. The findings were: majority of the sample populations were predisposed toward involvement in continuing education and to a lesser degree to distance education methods.

Westfall, Beth Davies (1991) developed a system to provide academic and non-academic support to the distance learners of Borandon University by an extensive surveying off-campus students. The results indicated that distance learners were on average older than their on-campus counterparts. Predominantly women, married having children, with a wide range of post-secondary educational experience. They were distance learners by necessity rather than by choice and feel that their support needs were not adequately met. In particular, they miss the interactive nature of on-campus learning and the free access to library resources and program information. Based on the findings, a model support service for distance learners was designed, pre-tested and recommended for implementation.

Roberts, Lowell Harlbut (1991) analyzed the self-reported learning goals and academic-self concepts of adult distance learners enrolled at the centre for distance learning of Empire State College by taking nine respondent characteristics: age, ethnicity, gender, income, major, distance education experience, previous education, years away from school, and educational plan. The results *inter-alia* include that the educational goals of distance students were found to be learning and career oriented. The goals most frequently cited as very important involved job skills, professional status, learning for its own sake and leadership skills. Distance students were not strongly self-confident of their academic abilities, tracts and skills. They did rate themselves very independent but they tendered to see themselves as average or below average in all other areas. They were most confident of their personal traits, such as independence, drive to achieve and persistence. They were least confident of specific skills such as those associated with interpreting poetry, solving mathematical problems and using a computer. Significant differences in self-concept strength were found by gender, income, distance education experience and major. In comparing distance education students with other adult students, the latter were found to be significantly more learning oriented. They were also significantly more self-confident across the full range of analyzed academic self-concepts, including personal traits, general academic abilities and specific academic skills.

Gee, Donna Beth Darter (1990) examined academic achievement, attitude, and course completion rates of twenty six graduate students in an on-campus and off-campus distance education classroom situation. It also examined the effect of students' preferred learning style on academic achievement, attitude and course completion rates. An analysis of co-variance showed no significant difference in on-campus and off-campus students' academic achievement. Results of 't' test showed no significant difference in on-campus and off-campus students' attitude. With all students completing the course, there was no significant difference in on-campus and off-campus students' course completion rates. Moreover, there was no difference in the course completion rates within the on-campus and off-campus learning style groups in academic achievement and attitude.

Suciati (1990) studied the effect of motivation on academic achievement in a distance education setting by studying a sample of 220 first semester open university students. The concept of motivation was measured by three factors: academic self-concept, expectancy of success and value of success. The persistence was measured by five factors: study hours, effort, tendency to do self-tests, intent to register and intent to succeed. Achievement was measured by the average achievement test score and the score for basic humanity. Inter correlations for all indicators of motivation, persistence and achievement showed that some factors of motivation correlated with persistence as well as achievement.

Murphy, Karen Lee (1990) analysed factors to which distance learners attribute their success and failure with in the system by studying a large number of students in the open education faculty (OEF). The results indicate that, in general, first year OEF students have a vocational orientation, and they use a surface approach that focuses primarily on memorizing information in their textbooks. They attribute both their success and failure primarily to a variety of conditions in their academic environments and to their own efforts; other success and failure attributions include luck and task difficulty. The experience of the first months in their new distance learning system challenges to these students. Most of the students enrolled were employed and typically older than first year students in other universities to conceive of their learning context in a different manner. As a result, they reconstruct or reconfigure a variety of elements in the system to meet their learning and social needs.

Gilroy, Lindsey (1989) conducted an extensive investigation into the entire distance learning system of a multi-national company with particular emphasis on the design, implementation, evaluation of materials, and the performance and attitudes of trainees were examined. The results indicted that trainees using distance learning had significantly higher test scores than trainees using conventional face to face training. Trainees with previous distance education experience were more likely to complete the course and with significantly higher scores than trainees with no previous experience. The more advanced the educational background of the trainers, the greater the likelihood of their completing the course.

Siqueira and Lynch (1986) studied the factors affecting student success at the National Open University of Venezuela by surveying a national sample of 521 students who had enrolled in the introductory course in 1980-81 which include 153 dropped out prior to the final examination, 114 failed in final examination and 254 successfully persisted. Chi-square and stepwise regression analysis were conducted to identify predictors of persistence and achievement. The chi-square analysis indicated the following variables were significantly related to academic outcome of non-traditional students: age, means of transportation, time devoted to study, use of personal instructional package, frequency of visits to local centres, concurrent attendance in other courses, working conditions while enrolled, main occupational activity perceptions of the difficulty of written materials, assignment load, quality of reading material, academic advising assistance, counselling assistance and satisfaction with the course. The stepwise multiple regression analysis indicated that four of the fifteen variables studied predicted 44 per cent of the variance in successful course completion, satisfaction with the course, frequency of visits to a local center, main professional activity while enrolled, and perception of the content of instructional material. Satisfaction with the course alone successfully predicted 28 per cent of the variance.

Phythian and Clements (1982) surveyed students who

withdrew from third level courses of British Open University. The respondents were asked to check three of twelve possible reasons for dropout. The most often reported reasons cited were: job (27%), domestic pressure (26%) and 'course too hard or long' (16%). From free-response comments it was apparent that one reason for high course dropout rates was a mismatch between the difficulty of the course and students' academic preparation. Lonliness and lack of support when they encountered difficulties also were the reasons for dropout.

Greenberg (1981) in his study expectancy theory predictions of completion behaviour and achievement in correspondence education sought to operationalize a method to predict likelihood of learners to complete a course. A stepwise regression analysis failed to confirm the expectancy model of motivation for course completion or course achievement. The most significant predictor of course achievement was high school grade point average, and the most significant predictor of course completion was correspondence study performance.

Willen, B. (1981) evaluated the experimental programme of distance education at Swedish Universities by collecting data from different sources like teachers, administrators, students and other planners of the universities. The findings *inter-alia* include a very high degree of satisfaction among participants and relatively high pass rates. Yet, the majority of the participants have kept a full time job besides their studies. A follow up study conducted on students of past five year period showed that the work situation was very stable for men but the women change work or work situation very frequently. The interest for continued education seems to be very high and 80 per cent of the group have been involved in some other kind of studies during the five year period.

Carr and Ledwith (1980) examined factors related to

success of disadvantaged adults beginning studies with the British Open University by taking a sample of 332 students who had dropped or failed, a random sample of 100 students who had completed their course-work and also a random sample of students interviewed by telephone. The results indicated that only one-fourth of the disadvantaged group received any academic counselling, two thirds of those who dropped out would have appreciated more assistance. The reasons stated by students who had withdrawn varied according to the course type. Those who enrolled in the arts and social sciences were more likely to cite personal or domestic problems where as those in math, science and technology courses cited job-oriented reasons.

Discussion and Conclusion

A bulk of research studies conducted in open and distance education both at national as well as international level have been reviewed in the preceding pages. Even though the learner, learner characteristics and their success are the issues for the present research, a number of diversified studies have been reviewed here, keeping in view the fact that each study has some direct or indirect bearing to the present work. An overview about these studies is given below.

Descriptive research studies focussing the concept, growth and development of distance and open education were carried out by many researchers (Biswal, 1979; Saini, 1979; Indiradevi, 1985; Mulay *et al.*, 1986; Bhattacharya, 1991; Singh *et al.*, 1993; etc.). Some researchers were interested in evaluating the distance education programmes/courses or institution as a whole (Jain, Pushpa Devi, 1991; Martin, 1991; Rathore, 1991; Sahoo, 1985; Pillai and Mohan, 1983; Gomati, 1982; Gilroy, Lindsey, 1980; Willen, B. 1981 etc.).

Efforts to findout the effectiveness of the distance education and open universities were also made by the researchers like Srivastava, Manjulika (1995), Vijaylakshmi (1994), Pugazhenthi (1991) and Upretti (1988). Use of media and technology, method of instruction and cost were also the focus of many researchers (Sesharatnam, 1994; Price, 1994; Powley, 1995; Iskandar, 1995; Hotrabhuvananada, 1992; Westfall, 1991; and Mishra, 1991).

The aspects of learners and their characteristics were a part of several studies. Some researches tried to find out the learners' characteristics, their background, motivation to join, expectations, satisfaction with course, anxieties, worry, problems of dropouts, study habits and learning skills (Pillai and Mohan 1984; Sahoo, 1985; Phythian, 1982; Suciati, 1990; Renu, 1990; Murphy, 1990; Carr and Ledwith, 1980; Das, 1992; Sang, 1994; Jegede *et al.*, 1992; Saga, 1993; Ekins, 1993; Roberts, L.H. 1990).

Researches are also being conducted to explore the academic performance, and factors contributing to the success in distance education system (Ram, 1984; Sahoo, 1985; Das, 1992; Renu, 1990; Siqueira and Lynch, 1986; Powley, 1995; Li-chun, 1995; Riddle, 1995 etc.). Certain learner variables have been identified as the predictors of success in learning system in some studies (Renu, 1990; Das, 1992; Riddle, 1995 and Siqueira and Lynch, 1986).

Empirical studies showing the relationship of attitudes of distance learners towards their courses/ studies and academic performance were also conducted by some researchers. A positive and significant relationship between academic performance has been reported by researchers like Sang (1994), Clark (1994), Smith, Dennie (1993) and Gee, Dona (1990).

On the basis of the above discussion it may be stated

safely that researches showing learner characteristics and their relation to the academic performance have been conducted only at a micro level particularly in the Indian context. Further the study of attitude have been only a part of many researches, and in almost in all researches these were examined in respect of the existing correspondence education. Hardly any study is available to show relationship between attitude of open university distance learners and their academic performance. The present piece of research is therefore an attempt towards filling up this research gap.

The design, plan and procedure adopted and method of execution, etc., of the study are dealt with in the following chapter.

CHAPTER 3

DESIGN OF THE STUDY

This chapter delineates the research design adopted for the present investigation. The main themes of this chapter revolves round the method used for investigation, variables involved in the study, nature and size of the sample selected for the present investigation, tools used for the collection of data, method of data collection and coding, and the statistical techniques employed for analysis and interpretation of the data.

The Method

The term 'Normative' implies the determination of normal or typical conditions, facts or practices. The term normative survey is generally used for the type of research, which proposes to ascertain what is the normal or typical condition or practice at the present time. The survey type of research is often confused with the mere gathering and tabulating the data while it goes beyond this. According to Best, "The Survey is an important type of study. It must not be confused with the mere clerical routine of gathering and tabulating figures. It involves a clearly defined problem and definite objectives. It requires expert and imaginative planning, careful analysis and interpretation of the data gathered and logical and skillful reporting of the findings" (Best, 1978).

In order to achieve the objectives of the present study Normative Survey method was used for investigating the inter-relationships among the variables *viz.*, academic self-concept, study habits, attitude towards distance education and academic performance.

Population

A population may refer to all of any specified groups of human being or of non-human entities such as objects, geographical areas, time units, methods, test or schools. The population selected for the present investigation is the distance learners who are undergoing the Bachelor's Degree Programme (BDP) of the Indira Gandhi National Open University (IGNOU), New Delhi under the jurisdiction of the IGNOU Regional Centre, Delhi.

The operational area of the IGNOU Regional Centre, Delhi includes the National Capital Territory of Delhi, two districts of Haryana, namely Gurgaon and Faridabad, Ghaziabad district and Modinagar town of Uttar Pradesh. The IGNOU Regional Centre, Delhi has got 23 study centres within an accessible distance of radius 25 kms. Further, most of the study centres are equipped with all modern facilities including facilities for teleconferencing at the Regional Centre. In addition to this, almost all distance learners have the access to Radio and Television. This provides the rationale to select the population from the IGNOU Regional Centre, Delhi. A detailed description of the BDP (Arts and Commerce) also been given in the first chapter.

Once the population is defined for the study, the next step is to select a representative sample from the population. It has been discussed in the following paragraphs.

The Sample

The population for the present study has been identified as the distance learners who are undergoing the BDP of the IGNOU Regional Centre, Delhi. The population has been further limited to the final year students of BDP (Arts and Commerce Stream) who have applied for the term end examination conducted in the month of December, 1994.

As per the address list provided by the computer centre of the IGNOU Regional Centre, Delhi, there were about 760 distance learners (B.A. and B.Com. stream only) applied for the term end examination conducted in December, 1994. It was decided to contact all the subjects covering the entire population. The responding subjects were considered as a random lot of candidates for inclusion in the sample.

The final sample for the present study consists of 318 distance learners of the IGNOU Regional Centre, Delhi. The sampling frame is summarized below in table 3.1.

Table 3.1

Sampling Frame
(First Degree Level Distance Learners)

Category	*Urban*	*Rural*	*Total*
Male	156	59	215
Female	93	10	103
Total	249	69	318

Description of Tools

The selection of suitable instruments or tools is of vital importance for successful research. As the study involved 3 main variables, namely, academic self-concept, study habits and attitude towards distance education, the following three tools were employed for measuring these three independent variables in the study.

(i) Academic Self-Concept Scale developed by the Researcher.

(ii) Study Habits Inventory for College Students developed by S.K. Jain (1967) (used with slight modification).

(iii) Attitude Scale towards Distance Education developed by the Researcher.

In addition to these three tools, a Personal Information Sheet was also developed and administered to get background information of the distance learners. A master sheet was prepared to collect information regarding the dependent variable 'Academic Performance' of distance learners, which were gathered from the Evaluation Division of the IGNOU, New Delhi. The tools are briefly described below.

(a) Personal Information Sheet

This has been developed to seek information regarding the background variables of distance learners. This includes the demographic variables like age, sex, marital status, locale, social class, employment status and the information pertaining to the course like year of admission, educational level, academic stream, previous experience in distance learning and discontinuity in studies.

(b) Academic Self-Concept Scale (ASCS)

Background

Self-concept is collequially defined as a composite view of one self. It is the way of looking at one self. It also signifies one's way of thinking, feeling and behaving. The sharp increase in the number of studies on self-concept is a reflection of the reemphasis on non-cognitive outcomes of education (Shavelson, *et al.* 1976). Further, many of the self-concept studies have shown a positive and significant relationship with academic achievement (Shanmugan Sundaram, 1983; Singh, 1983; Sween, 1984; Pathni, 1985; Saraswat, 1982; Padhi, 1992; Sylves, 1993; Cazenave, 1993). Considerable body of literature is now available which deals with the nature of self-concept, components of self-concept, types of self-concept, development of self-concept. Further, Shavelson, *et al.* (1976) identified a number of distinctive features of self-concept: *(i)* organised, *(ii)* multifaceted, *(iii)* hierarchical, *(iv)* stable (general self-concept)/unstable (situational), *(v)* developmental, *(vi)* descriptive and evaluative and *(vii)* differentiable from other constructs.

Shift from General Self-Concept to Academic Self-Concept

Recent self-concept theories emphasizes the multi-dimentionality of self-concept (Shavelson, *et al.* 1976; Byrne and Shavelson, 1986; Marsh, Byrne and Shavelson, 1988; Shavelson, Hubner and Stanton, 1976). Shavelson, *et al.* 1976, proposed a general self-concept defined by academic and non-academic self-concept. Academic self-concept was divided into self-concept in particular content areas, and non-academic self-concept was divided social, physical and emotional self-concepts.

Further, the research studies in self-concept concluded with the fact that the general/global self-concept was weakly correlated with academic achievement and confirmed the higher correlation between the academic self-concept and academic performance (Marsh and Parker, 1984; Shavelson and Bolus, 1982; Hansford and Hattie, 1982; Mc Cabe, 1992; Marsh, 1993; Saraswat, 1982; Radha Rani, 1983; Bachman, 1970; Byrne, 1984; Marsh, *et al.* 1985). Moreover, achievement in particular content areas to be mostly correlated with self-concept in the matching content areas (Marsh, *et al.*, 1985).

Rationale for Construction of ASCS

Since most of the tools available for measurement of self-concept/academic self-concept were mainly on the formal school students' self-concept and many of them were constructed exclusively for young children, obvious need for constructing a scale for academic self-concept of adult distance learners was felt.

Construction of ASCS

Dr.(Mrs.) M.R. Rastogi (1979) developed a 'Likert Type' Self-Concept Scale . The researcher also followed the same pattern for developing the academic self-concept scale. Various steps involved in the construction of the Academic Self-Concept Scale are described in the following paragraphs.

Selection of Items

Academic Self-Concept has been defined for the present study as the experience of one's own being so far as the academic concerns are involved. It includes what people come to know about themselves through experience, attention and feedback from others especially in relation to academic aspects. The investigator scanned several such scales developed by Indian and foreign authors. A collection of items was thus developed and discussed with the experts in the area in and outside NCERT. Their comments were sought item wise and the list were reviewed on the basis of feedback received. A set of 71 items was finally proposed for Academic Self-Concept Scale commensurate with the adult learners characteristics.

Preliminary Form of the Scale

The preliminary Academic Self-Concept Scale comprised of 71 items of Likert type on five point rating scale. Each of the items were provided with alternative responses such as Strongly Agree (SA), Agree (A), Undecided (UD), Disagree (D) and Strongly Disagree (SD). It was a self-administering tool without any time limit. The scoring was done on the basis of a five-point scale. For a positive item a weightage of 5,4,3,2,1 were given to SA, A, UD, D and SD respectively. Similarly for a negative item a weightage of 1,2,3,4,5 were given to SA, A, UD, D and SD respectively. The summated score of all the seventy items provide the total academic self-concept score of an individual. The maximum possible score on the whole scale could be 350 and the minimum score as 70. A high score indicates a higher self-concept, while a low score shows low self-concept.

Pre-try out

After selecting the items for the scale, the scale was pre-tried out on 10-15 distance learners in a study centre at Delhi in order to find out the difficulties of the learners in responding to the items and understanding the language, etc. After this preliminary administration, screening and editing of the items was done. Efforts were also made to improve the language and removing ambiguity in understanding the items.

Try out

The academic self-concept scale was then administered to 130 distance learners of the IGNOU attending various study centres situated in different parts of Delhi. Care was taken to include BDP distance learners with varying backgrounds. After getting responses, they were scored for each individual separately.

Item Analysis

Item analysis has been carried to screen out better kind the items. Item discrimination was ascertained by applying 't' test on the performance of high and low groups formed. On the basis of the total scores, *i.e.* 27 per cent of the high scorers (High group) and 27 per cent of the low scorers (Low group) out of the total group were identified. Then their scored responses in terms of weighted scores for each item were worked out. To find out the extent to which a given item differentiates between the high and the low groups or to find out the discriminating values of the items, 't' test was applied for each of the 71 items. Only the items showing significant difference between their mean scores of high and low groups of 0.05 level were included in the final form of the Academic Self-Concept Scale. The rest of the items were rejected besides few of them (marginal cases) were modified suitably.

The Final Form of the Scale

The final form of the Academic Self-Concept Scale consists of 40 items measuring 8 dimensions of academic self-concept. The scale consists of 15 positive items and 25 negative items. Each item in the scale is provided with five possible alternative responses such as Strongly Agree (SA), Agree (A), Undecided (UD), Disagree (D) and Strongly Disagree (SD). Dimensionwise distribution of items is provided below in table 3.2.

Table 3.2

Distribution of Items in Eight Dimensions of the Academic Self-Concept Scale

S. No.	*Dimensions of ASC*	*S.No. of Statements on the Scale*	*Total No. of Items*
1.	Academic Abilities and Interest	1,2,3,4,6,8,9,10	8
2.	Self-Confidence in Course	22,23,24,25,36,	5
3.	Academic Interaction	11, 21, 32	3
4.	Study Preparation	5, 7, 12, 18, 19, 34, 40	7
5.	Academic Time	13, 14, 15, 16, 17	5
6.	Academic Future	26, 27, 33	3
7.	Examination	20, 28, 29, 30	4
8.	Mode of Study	31, 35, 37, 38, 39	5
	Total		40

Administration of the Scale

The Academic Self-Concept Scale is a self-administering tool. This scale is mainly used for adults who are pursuing any course or study through distance mode of education provided by the Open Universities or the Directorates of Distance Education of Conventional Universities. There is no time limit for the test. However, normally an adult learner takes 30 minutes to complete all the items.

The following specific instructions were given to the respondents. "Here are some statements relating to your academic and educational aspects. Each statement is associated with five possibilities of your responses, *viz.*, Strongly Agree (SA), Agree (A), Undecided (UD), Disagree (D) and Strongly Disagree (SD). Please go through each statement carefully and give your response by ticking (✓) on any one of the five responses given".

Reliability

Reliability of a tool may be defined as the extent to which a tool is consistent in measuring whatever it does measure. It expresses the consistency of scores on a test. For the present tool only split-half reliability was calculated for practical academic considerations.

Split-half Reliability

The tool is first divided into two equivalent 'halves'. The procedure followed in the present study had odd numbered items included in first half and even numbered items in second half. The measure of the first half of the tool was then correlated with the measure of the other half. The correlation coefficients of the measures of two half was found to be 0.80. Then the reliability coefficient of the total tool was calculated using Spearman - Brown prophecy formula $r_{tt} = 2r/1+r$.

Where 'rtt' is the reliability coefficient of the total test and 'r' is the coefficient of correlation between two halves of the test.

Hence rtt = 2x0.80/1+0.80
= 1.60/1.80 = 0.89

Thus the obtained reliability score through split-half method seems to be quite acceptable for the Academic Self-Concept Scale. Further, the consistency among the scores in eight dimensions and the total score was quite satisfactory as coefficients of correlations ranged from 0.22 to 0.79. It indicates the unitary nature of the academic self-concept scale.

Validity

Validity refer to the extent to which a tool measures for which it is intended to measure. This term has different connotations for various types of tools and, thus, a different type of validity evidence is appropriate for each. For validating the present tool, face and content validities have been ensured.

Face Validity and Content Validity

Face validity was ensured through careful collection of the items for the academic self-concept scale. Further, the content validity was established through expert judgement on the scale and the discussion with educational psychologists of the National and International repute.

Norms

Raw score norms have been attempted for interpretation of the results. The norms have been developed on the total sample of 318 BDP distance learners at the first degree level. No attempt has been made to give norms for sex-wise or any other classification. The table 3.3 shows the raw score norms to the total self-concept score.

Table 3.3

Raw Score Norms for Academic Self-Concept Scale

Classification	*Range of Scores*
High ASC	161-200
Above Average ASC	121-160
Average ASC	81-120
Below Average ASC	41-80
Low ASC	1-40

(c) Study Habits Inventory

This inventory was developed by Dr. S.K. Jain (1967) in Hindi to measure the study habits of college and university going students of Uttar Pradesh. The inventory measures the study habits of an individual in 8 areas. A description of these areas are presented below.

(i) Understanding Habits : This indicate the students' urge to understand the reading materials. It includes the modes of reading and grasp of the student over the subject and ways adopted by him/her in understanding a particular work.

(ii) Planning Habits : This shows the student's overall plan of his/her study programme throughout the year in general and during the examination period in particular. It reflects whether the student's approach to studies is haphazard or well planned so that he/she can study all subjects efficiently.

(iii) Working Habits : It shows whether the student is regular in study and has been continuously trying to complete the day to day work. It also covers the efforts put in by him/her during the examination time.

(iv) Notes-taking Habits : It reveals different ways and means followed a student in taking notes from the reading materials; and making chart, graph, etc., for better understanding.

(v) Concentration Habits : It reflects to the fact whether the student successfully focuses his/her attention to lectures or reading the material. The ways which students adopt for better concentration and the sources interrupting their concentration at particular study time are included in this category.

(vi) Interest in Studies : This area shows students' interest towards their studies and course. Further, it also indicate students attitude towards difficult and boring subject matter and other co-curricular activities.

(vii) Memorizing Habits : This shows the ways adopted by the student for learning the material, for better retention and to review what he/she has learnt for facilitating recall.

(viii) Consultation Habits : It indicate the extent to which a student seeks help from others in his/her studies and utilizes such help to his/her advantage. It also covers whether he/she hesitates to discuss his/her difficulties with colleagues, counsellors/teachers, etc.

This inventory was developed for the undergraduate and post-graduate arts students. The original Hindi version of the inventory contains 80 items. However, in the light of the present sample, the inventory has been adapted to suit the requirements of distance learners. Unlike formal education, in distance learning or teaching there is no classroom as such, some of the items focussing the classroom aspects have been eliminated in the modified version. The modified version contains 55 items only.

Functional Reliability and Validity of the Modified Study Habits Inventory

The original form of the Study Habits Inventory had the reliability indices of 0.907 and 0.91 for split-half and test retest reliabilities respectively. The author has quoted validity indices of 0.697 and 0.597 against the criterion of teachers' ratings and examination marks. Since this tool was modified for the distance learners, an attempt was made to establish the reliability and validity afresh as described in the following paragraphs:

Reliability

The reliability of the modified version of the inventory was calculated through split-half method. The odd numbered and even numbered items were separated into two halves then the coefficient of correlation between the two halves scores was calculated. The coefficients of correlation was found to be r=0.89. Then the reliability of the total score was calculated using Spearman-Brown prophecy formula described earlier. Thus the reliability coefficients of the total test was found to be 0.94. Which showed a high reliability measure. The internal consistency was also examined through inter correlations among 8 areas of the study habits and to the total score which ranged form 0.14 to 0.85

Validity

Face validity and content validity of the study habits inventory was assured through experts judgement of 5 experts as the test items were taken from the standardized study habits inventory.

Norms

Raw score norms have been prepared for interpretation of the scores on Study Habits Inventory. The norms are prepared to the total sample of the first degree level distance learners and are presented in table 3.4.

Table 3.4

Raw Score Norms for Study Habits Inventory

Classification	*Range of Raw Scores*
Effective SH	166-220
Good SH	111-165
Poor SH	56-110
Defective SH	0-55

Administration

The study habits inventory is a self administrative tool. It can be administered individually as well as in group. There is no time limit, but normally 30-40 minutes may take by a respondent to attempt all the items.

Before administration of the inventory the following instructions were given to the respondents. "Here are some statements regarding your study related activities. Each statement is associated with four possibilities of your responses *viz.*, Never (N), Sometimes (ST), Mostly (MS) and Always (AL). Please go through each statement carefully and give your response by ticking (✓) any one of the four responses given."

Scoring Procedure

The inventory consists both positive as well as negative statements. The respondent is provided with four alternatives to each statement, namely, Never, Sometimes, Mostly and Always. For each positive item a score of one to four and for each negative item a score of four to one respectively is given, and adding all these scores provides the total study habits score of an individual.

(d) Attitude Scale Towards Distance Education

Introduction

Attitude is normally defined as a generalized pattern in

perception or action towards an object or thing as in integration of various experience. In the beginning of the twentieth century itself, psychologists started defining 'attitude' in many ways. However, Allport (1935) identified three main features of attitude as: *(a)* preparation or readiness for favourable or unfavourable responses, *(b)* which is organised through experience, and *(c)* which is activated in the presence of all objects and situations with which the attitude is related. Again, Fishbein and Ajzen (1975) also provides three essential features of attitude. According to them, 'attitude is learned... it pre-disposes action, and such actions are consistently favourable or unfavourable towards the object". These two attempts clearly helps to understand what attitude is.

Measurement of Attitude

Thurstone boldly asserted that 'attitude can be measured'. Attempts to measure attitude require making of inferences about attitude from some observable indicator. The most commonly used method that enables inference to be made is based on individual's responses to a series of sentences or adjectives presented in the form of a scale. The most frequently used scales are Likert Scale, Thurston Scale, Guttman Scale, and Semantic Differential Scale. These scales are widely used in educational research for the measurement of attitude.

Students' Attitude Towards Studies

Pupil and teacher attitude studies are quite common in behavioural sciences. In the field of education, among the various affective correlates of academic achievements, attitude towards various areas of Education (school, studies, learning, subjects, etc.) figured as an important attribute. Various researchers in the field of education have tried to show the relationship between attitude towards school/studies and academic achievement. Thus it highlights the importance of developing desirable attitude towards studies for the success in education.

Attitude Towards Distance Education

Even though, distance education is a very recent phenomenon, a large number of studies have been conducted to know the learners, teachers and society's attitude towards this innovative mode of education. In the Indian context, only a few micro level studies have been attempted to measure distance learners' attitude towards distance education. They all become only a part of their studies (for example: Pillai, 1984; Khan, 1982; Ram, 1984; Sahoo, 1985; Sahoo and Bhat, 1987; Panda and Choudhary, 1989; Renu, 1990; Pandey, 1991; Nagpal, 1992, etc.). Moreover, they were limited in their scope and range.

Rationale for Construction of Attitude Scale Towards Distance Education

A review of attitude studies in the field of distance education revealed that most of the tools prepared were focussed on the existing correspondence education prevailing in those days. However, establishment of National and State level Open Universities changed remarkably the method of instruction and student support services to the distance learners. In this changed scenario, it was very essential to develop a comprehensive tool, which would measure the distance learners' attitude towards distance education in a variety of dimensions. Thus the researcher made an attempt in this direction. The actual construction procedures are explained in the following paragraphs keeping in view the steps suggested by Edwards, 1969.

Rationale for Using Likert Scale

Among the different techniques available for the construction of attitude scale, the more popularly used techniques are : *(a)* the method of equal appearing intervals known as the 'Thurstone technique' and *(b)* the method of summated rating popularly known as 'Likert technique'. These two methods are widely used in Educational Research. Each technique has some advantages over the other. However, Likert's technique was preferred in the present tool construction as there is a scope for the expression of intensity of an opinion through the scaled response besides being easy to construct.

Likert scales consist of a series of statements, all of which are related to a person's attitude towards a single object. Two types of statements that appear on Likert scales are : *(i)* favourable statements, and *(ii)* unfavourable statements. An approximately equal number of favourable and unfavourable statements, typically, are included on a likert scale. The procedure followed for the construction of Likert type attitude scale is described below :

Collection of Items

The researcher first enlisted all possible areas/scope of distance education. Then consulted the recent literature available as well as with the professors, teachers and counsellors (working in the field of distance education) from the IGNOU, NCERT, NIEPA, AIU, NOS, etc., for writing the items. Previous small scale studies, like that of the project work of the students of Diploma in Distance Education offered by IGNOU, some M.Ed., M.Phil. dissertations and Ph.D. theses in the area of distance education were also consulted to cull out the items for the attitude scale. These items were then discussed with the experts in the field at different intervals to determine the relevance of items to be included in each category in order to avoid replication. Efforts were made to improve the language and to remove ambiguity to make them understandable to the learners in its first reading. The collected items were thoroughly screened and edited. Thus a total of 100 items were included in the draft attitude scale.

The Preliminary Form of the Scale

After preliminary screening and editing of the statements and their pretry-out and modification, the preliminary form of the attitude scale comprised 100 items of Likert type on a five point rating scale. Each items, therefore, contained five alternative responses such as Strongly Agree (SA), Agree (A), Undecided (UD), Disagree (D), and Strongly Disagree (SD). It was a self administering tool without any time limit. The scoring was based on a five point Likert type scale designed for a positive item weighed a score of 5 for SA, 4 for A, 3 for UD, 2 for D and 1 for SD and for a negative item 1 for SA, 2 for A, 3 for UD, 4 for D and 5 for SD. The summated score of all the 100 items provide the total attitude score. Thus the maximum possible score on the whole attitude scale is 500 and the minimum possible score is 100. A high score on the scale indicates a favourable attitude, while a low score shows an unfavourable attitude towards distance education.

Try out

The attitude scale was administered to a group of 140 BDP distance learners of the IGNOU by visiting various study centres of the IGNOU situated in the National Capital Territory, Delhi. Proper sampling procedure was followed to select distance learners from each zone and from varied categories like employed/unemployed, male/female and experience in distance education, etc. The responses were collected and scored for each individual separately.

Item Analysis

Item analysis was carried out to eliminate inconsistency of the items. The responses of the subjects were scored by allotting weightage to the items as described in the previous page. The weighted score for each item, and also for each subject, was totalled up. On the basis of the total scores, 27% of the high scores (High group) and 27% of the low scores (Low group) among the group were identified. Their scored responses in terms of weighted scores for each item were tabulated separately for high and low groups and the mean score for each item were worked out. Item analysis was carried on by using 't' test for each of the 100 statements for the higher and lower group. Thus the significance of difference between the means were worked out to find out the discriminating power of each items; how well each item can distinguish between individuals having different attitudes. Only those items, which showed a significant difference between high and low groups, were selected to for inclusion in the final form of the test.

Final Form of the Scale

The final form of the attitude scale consists of 70 statements in 8 dimensions of distance education. There are 30 positive statements and 40 negative statements. The distribution of items in the 8 domains is presented in table 3.5. Each item in the attitude scale is provided with five possible alternative responses such as Strongly Agree (SA), Agree (A), Undecided (UD), Disagree (D) and Strongly Disagree (SD).

Table 3.5

Distribution of Items in Eight Domains of Attitude Scale Towards Distance Education

S. No.	*Domains of Attitude*	*S.No. of Statements on the Scale*	*Total No. of Items*
1.	General	1,2,3,4,5,6,7,8,9,10	10
2.	Admission Procedures	11,12,13,14,15	5
3.	Self-Instructional Material (Print)	16,17,18,19,20,21, 22,23,24,25	10
4.	Multi-Media Instruction	26,27,28,29,30,31, 32,33,34	9
5.	Assignments	35,36,37,38,39,40, 41,42,43, 44	10
6.	Counselling Sessions	45,46,47,48,49,50, 51,52,53	9
7.	Study Centres	54,55,56,57,58,59, 60,61	8
8.	Evaluation System	62,63,64,65,66,67, 68,69,70	9
Total			70

Administration of the Scale

The attitude scale is a self-administered tool. This scale is mainly used for adults who are pursuing their studies through distance education provided by the open universities or the Directorates of distance education of conventional universities where a multi-media instruction is prevalent. There is no time limit for the test. However, normally distance learners take 30 to 45 minutes to respond all the items.

The following specific instructions were given to the respondents, "Here are some statements pertaining to various aspects of distance education. Each statement is associated with five possibilities of your response, *viz.*, Strongly Agree (SA), Agree (A), Undecided (UD), Disagree (D) and Strongly Disagree (SD). Please go through each statement carefully and give your response by ticking (✓) on any one of the five given responses."

Reliability

For the present attitude scale only split-half reliability was calculated. In order to obtain the split-half reliability, the test was administered only once and then divided into two halves by having all the odd-numbered items into first half and all the even-numbered items into second half. Thus two parallel halves containing 35 items each were obtained. The coefficient of correlation between the two halves was calculated. It was found that the coefficient of correlation between the scores of two halves was r=0.84. Then the reliability coefficient of the total test was calculated using Spearman-Brown prophecy formula

$$rtt = 2r/1+r$$

where 'rtt' is the reliability coefficient of the total test and 'r' is the coefficient of correlation between two halves of the test.

$$\text{Hence } rtt = 2x0.84/1+0.84$$
$$= 1.68/1.84$$
$$rtt = 0.91$$

Thus, the reliability score obtained through split-half method was found to be high and much faith can be placed in the results obtained through this scale. Further, internal consistency between the scores on 8 domains and the total scores was also examined to substantiate the reliability index of the scale. The matrix of coefficients of correlations between the scores of 8 domains and to the total scores on the attitude scale shows that the minimum correlation value is 0.28 and maximum correlation value is 0.77. All the 36 values of correlation coefficients have been found to be significant at 0.01 level. Thus the coefficient of correlation matrix provides sufficient evidence for the high internal consistency of scores on 8 domains of Attitude Scale.

Face Validity and Content Validity

In the present attitude scale an attempt has been made to ensure face validity and content validity through consultation with experts from the IGNOU, NCERT and NIEPA from the very beginning of identifying the statements to the final selection of the statements. Thus on the basis of constructive comments by the experts, the items were modified/eliminated. Thus the face validity and content validity were duly ensured to some extent.

Norms

For the interpretation of the scores on attitude scale towards distance education raw score norms have been prepared to the total sample. Table 3.6 shows the raw score norms on the total attitude score.

Table 3.6

Raw Score Norms for Attitude Scale Towards Distance Education

Interpretation	*Range of Raw Scores*
High ADE	281-350
Above Average ADE	211-280
Average ADE	141-210
Below Average ADE	71-140
Low ADE	1-70

Indicators of Academic Performance

The data with respect to the dependent variable 'Academic Performance' has been collected from the marks registers maintained by the Evaluation Division of the IGNOU with the cooperation and permission of the authorities. Academic performance of distance learners who are enrolled in the year 1991 were only selected for the study to have control over the duration of the study and their performance. Further, the university provides a maximum of 8 years to complete the BDP of IGNOU as such; it is just possible that the distance learners enrolled in 1991 may still be continuing the course. Thus a measure of 'Academic Performance' needs to be developed keeping this issue in mind. When going through the performance of distance learners enrolled in the year 1991, it was found that only very limited number of distance learners have successfully completed the course. Further, majority of them cleared certain courses and still struggling with the remaining courses. However, few of them could not clear even a single course. Even then, one can not stick them as failures as the university give much autonomy to complete their course at their own pace.

Keeping the nature of progress of the learners in distance education, the researcher formulated an "indicator" as a measure of Academic Performance, which is based on the following procedures. In fact, the BDP programme is of a 96 credit course in 3 major categories as: *(i)* Foundation Courses, *(ii)* Elective Courses, and *(iii)* Application Oriented Courses. (Details are presented in the first chapter). In each of these 3 major categories, there are various courses. Each course is having a weightage of 8 credit and some others are having a weightage of 4 credits or 2 credit. In fact, the maximum possible score of the 8 credit course is 100 and that of a 4 credit, it is 50 and 2 credit, it is 25. As such the 96 credit course's total maximum possible score is 1200.

For successful completion of a course, a learner has to acquire a required minimum percentage in the assignments (which has a weightage of 30 per cent to the total) and the term end examination (of a weightage of 70 per cent) in a particular course. The letter grade and percentages are calculated separately for assignments and term end examination and then added together to have the final grade and percentage.

For the present research, the percentage of marks obtained for the courses in which the learner has been successfully completed are taken. Then these were added together and computed to get the final percentage out of the maximum possible score of 1200. The obtained value is considered as the indicator of the academic performance of distance learners. The calculated percentage was found to be ranging from 1.8 to 67.97.

Procedure of Data Collection

First of all the researcher approached the IGNOU Regional Director (Delhi) to get the mailing list of these learners and also to get a covering letter to the distance learners under the study.

There were about 760 learners, who had applied for the term-end examination held in December, 1994. The tool booklet was sent to all the 760 distance learners. The tool booklet contained three tools namely, academic self-concept scale, study habits inventory and attitude scale towards distance education and the personal information form. Further, a general instruction was also given in addition to the toolwise specific instructions. The space to mark the responses was also provided against each statement. The set of general instructions printed at the top of the booklet read as: *(i)* Give your response by ticking (✓) the appropriate answers in the following proforma, *(ii)* Do not leave any statement without answering, *(iii)* Do not write any thing on the box given in the left side (in fact, this box is provided for coding purpose), *(iv)* Your responses will be kept strictly confidential and used for research purpose only.

The tools were prepared both in Hindi and English. Hindi and English Versions of tools were printed separately. An English version of the tool is presented in

Appendix. Hindi tools were sent to majority of the distance learners. However, for a selected non-Hindi learners (as noted from office records) the English version was also sent. Along with the tool booklet, self addressed and stamped envelopes were also attached therewith for sending back the filled in tool booklet.

The initial response was very poor. However, with a number of repeated reminders, the researcher could get back a total of about 325 tool booklets. The mailing of the tool booklets started in the month of May, 1995 and completed in the month of September, 1995. There were about 7 booklets incomplete and partially attempted. These were not counted for scoring purpose. Thus the final sample consisted of 318 distance learners. The responses to personal information sheet/background information and for the 3 tools were then computed through using a particular coding method.

Coding of Data

As the analysis of the present research was to be done with the help of computer in the SPSS package, the responses received were coded properly before sending them to the computer centre. Coding on the 3 tools were made against the responses to each statement. The scale value is considered as the code for a particular statement. Further, suitable codes were also given to the background informations. Thus the total scores, sub scores on subtests and scores based on background variables of distance learners for each tool were made available after analysis through the SPSS. The calculated percentage as the indicator/measure of Academic Performance was used as for the analysis purposes.

Statistical Techniques Used

The following statistical techniques were employed for analysis of the data:

(i) *Percentage* : Percentage was used mainly to analyse the background characteristics of distance learners.

(ii) *Mean and Standard Deviation (SD)* : Mean scores and SDs were calculated to know the level of academic self-concept, study habits and attitude towards distance education of the selected sample of distance learners.

(iii) *'t' test/C.R. Values* : C.R. values were compute to know the significance of difference between the mean scores of distance learners on three independent variables namely academic self-concept, study habits and attitude towards distance education differing in their background variables.

(iv) *Pearsons' Product Moment Correlation* : Pearsons' Product Moment Correlation Coefficients were computed to determine the relationship between the 3 independent variable, namely, academic self-concept, study habits and attitude towards distance education with the academic performance of distance learners.

(v) *Multiple Correlation and Multiple Linear Regression Equations* : Multiple Correlation and Regression Equations were used to determine the degree of prediction of academic performance of distance learners (dependent/criterion variable) by treating academic self-concept, study habits and attitude towards distance education as independent/explanatory variables.

The analysis and interpretation of the data in the context of the objectives and hypotheses of the study have been attempted in the following chapter.

CHAPTER 4

ANALYSIS AND INTERPRETATION OF DATA

The previous chapter provides details about the design of the study, methodology adopted, the sampling frame, description of tools used, procedure of data collection and coding and a brief account of relevant statistical techniques used in the study.

The present chapter has been devoted to the analysis and interpretation of the data in the context of the objectives and hypotheses of the study.

In pursuance of the objectives of the study the obtained data were tabulated, classified and analysed to yield meaningful interpretation of results which may eventually lead to significant findings of the study.

The analysis and interpretation of the results of the study have been presented in six parts. In the first part, the background characteristics of the distance learners have been examined and interpreted. Part two deals with the nature of data with respect to the academic self-concept, study habits and attitude of first degree distance learners towards distance education for the total sample *vis-a-vis* their characteristics.

Part three provides the study of the significance of mean differences in academic self-concept, study habits and attitude towards distance education among the distance learners with varying background.

Part four speaks of the nature of relationship obtaining between the dependent variable, namely, the academic performance of distance learners and the concerned independent variables *e.g.*, academic self-concept, study habits and attitude towards distance education.

The fifth part of analysis attempts to predict academic performance of first degree level distance learners on the basis of their academic self-concept, study habits and attitude towards distance education. The sixth and last part suggests the various ways of enhancing academic performance of first degree level distance learners.

PART ONE

BACKGROUND CHARACTERISTICS OF DISTANCE LEARNERS

This part look into the background characteristics of the sampled distance learners of first degree level in terms of their academic and socio-economic backgrounds. This part caters to the first objective and hypothesis of the study which are stated below.

Objective 1

'To assess the background characteristics of the first degree level distance learners of Delhi and adjoining areas'.

Hypothesis 1

'First degree level distance learners may be found to vary with regard to academic and socio-economic backgrounds'.

The analysis of the background characteristics of the first degree distance learners was made on the following eleven variables : *(i)* Year of Enrolment, *(ii)* Sex, *(iii)* Age, *(iv)* Marital Status, *(v)* Locale, *(vi)* Social Class, *(vii)* Academic Stream, *(viii)* Educational Level, *(ix)* Employment Status, *(x)* Experience in Distance Learning, and *(xi)* Discontinuity in Studies. These have been discussed itemwise in the following paragraphs.

(i) Distribution of Learners by Year of Enrolment

Since the IGNOU provides a minimum of 3 years and a maximum of 8 years to complete the Bachelor's Degree Programme (BDP) , it is quite natural that learners with different years of enrolment might have appeared for term end examination conducted in December, 1994 which is a point of reference for the study. Table 4.1 provides details of the subjects (distance learners) with regard to their year of enrolment.

Table 4.1

Distribution of Learners by Year of Enrolment

Category	*Number of Learners*	*Percentage*
1988	9	2.8
1989	38	11.9
1990	56	17.6
1991	215	67.7
Total	318	100

Table 4.1 reveals that majority of the sampled distance learners (67.7%) were enrolled in the year 1991. However, 17.6 per cent learners were enrolled in 1990, 11.9 per cent and 2.8 per cent in the years 1989 and 1988 respectively. Thus the data revealed that the distance learners enrolled in 1988 onwards were still pursuing the BDP even at the end of December, 1994 because of the flexibility in studies provided by the Open University. About 32 per cent of distance learners were there who could not reach the final year even after 4 to 6 years of enrolment to BDP.

(ii) Distribution of Learners by Sex

One of the objectives of the open universities is to give access to women and other disadvantaged groups to higher and further education. The distribution of male and female distance learners at the first degree level (BDP) has been provided in table 4.2.

Table 4.2

Distribution of Learners by Sex

Category	*Number of Learners*	*Percentage*
Male	215	67.6
Female	103	32.4
Total	318	100

It is evident from the above table that a high proportion (67.6%) of first degree level distance learners were males. Only 32.4 per cent learners were females in the sample of distance learners taken for the study. However, the female percentage in the first degree level was relatively high as compared to the total enrolment of females in the IGNOU programmes which happens to be 22.5 per cent only as on January 1995 (Takwale, 1995).

(iii) Distribution of Learners by Age

Unlike the conventional universities we do find learners with different age groups pursuing studies through distance mode. In the present study, learners were asked to indicate their age in any one of the two categories, namely, below 25 years and 25 years and above. The data in this regard are presented in table 4.3.

An inspection of table 4.3 would reveal that in the age-wise distribution of first degree level distance learners majority of the learners (70.8%) were older than 25 years of the age. The rest of them (29.2%) were below 25 years in age. Thus the data reveals that the first degree level programmes of the IGNOU have attracted relatively mature group of adults.

Table 4.3

Distribution of Learners by Age

Category	*Number of Learners*	*Percentage*
Below 25	93	29.2
25 and above	225	70.8
Total	318	100

(iv) Distribution of Learners by Marital Status

Unlike the conventional universities, many married learners pursue their studies through open and distance learning. As far as the marital status of the first degree distance learners is concerned, the data are presented in table 4.4.

Table 4.4

Distribution of Learners by Marital Status

Category	*Number of Learners*	*Percentage*
Married	162	50.9
Unmarried	156	49.1
Total	318	100

Table 4.4 reveals that more than half of the learners (50.9%) were married ones in the sampled lot of distance learners. The percentage of unmarried learners were also around 50 per cent (49.1%). This shows that almost an equal number of married and unmarried learners take up the first degree programmes of IGNOU.

(v) Distribution of Learners by Locale

Providing equal educational opportunities for the rural

and remote area people is one of the objectives of the open universities. The rural and urban distribution of the sampled distance learners are presented in the following table :

Table 4.5

Distribution of Learners by Locale

Category	*Number of Learners*	*Percentage*
Urban	249	78.3
Rural	69	21.7
Total	318	100

The location-wise distribution of the distance learners shows a high concentration of (78.3%) urban distance learners in the first degree level programmes of IGNOU.

This high concentration of distance learners in urban area may be attributable to some extent to the fact that the samples were drawn from the IGNOU Regional Centre, Delhi. As per 1991 Census, the state of Delhi has only about 10 per cent rural population. However, about 20 per cent of learners reported that they belonged to rural areas; may be they would be living in the border areas and in the adjoining states of Delhi.

(vi) Distribution of Learners by Social Class

The Indian society comprises of various castes and cultural groups. In the present study, distance learners were asked to categorize themselves into two groups : *(i)* SC/ST, *(ii)* Non SC/ST. The Non SC/ST learners include OBCs and other general castes/classes. Table 4.6 provides the distribution of learners in these two categories.

Table 4.6

Distribution of Learners by Social Class

Category	*Number of Learners*	*Percentage*
SC/ST	61	19.2
Non SC/ST	257	80.8
Total	318	100

The data in table 4.6 reveals that the representation of SC/ST was to the tune of 19.2 per cent. The remaining 80.8 per cent learners were either of general or OBC category. According to Takwale (1995), the enrolment of SC/ST learners as on 1st January, 1995 was 7 per cent in the total IGNOU programmes. However, the present data show a high percentage of SC/ST concentration in the BDP.

(vii) Distribution of Learners by Academic Streams

Learners with Arts stream and Commerce stream were only taken for the present study. Table 4.7 provides the distribution of sampled first degree learners with respect to their academic stream. The summarized version is reported in table 4.7.

Table 4.7

Distribution of Learners by Academic Streams

Category	*Number of Learners*	*Percentage*
B.A.	258	81.1
B.Com.	60	18.9
Total	318	100

It may be noted from the above table that majority (81.1%) of the first degree level distance learners come from arts stream. The percentage oi commerce based learners was only around 20. Perhaps the BDP has gained popularity amongst arts learners and other streams have yet to make efforts to make their programme acceptable to learners of other streams.

(viii) Distribution of Learners by Educational Level

Distance learners with formal qualification (+2 or equivalent) and without any formal qualification are admitted to the BDP of the IGNOU. Those who do not have +2 or equivalent qualification have to go through Bachelor's Preparatory Programme (BPP) before getting admitted to the BDP. The distribution of the sampled distance learners' level of previous education is presented in table 4.8.

Table 4.8

Distribution of Learners by Educational Level

Category	*Number of Learners*	*Percentage*
+2 or Equivalent	152	47.8
Non +2	166	52.2
Total	318	100

More than half (52%) of the sampled distance learners were not having any formal qualification (Non+2) at the time of enrolment to the BDP. Only 47.8 per cent learners had +2 or equivalent level of education before seeking admission to the BDP. Thus the data shows that the first degree programmes of IGNOU have attracted more of the learners without +2 or equivalent certificate. It seems to fulfil one of the aim of the open universities to provide access to higher education to all its aspirants.

(ix) Distribution of Learners by Employment Status

The open universities have a premise of attracting the employed workers to upgrade their qualifications, develop skills and uptodating their knowledge. Table 4.9 provides the employment status of the first degree distance learners in the sample of study.

Table 4.9

Distribution of Learners by Employment Status

Category	*Number of Learners*	*Percentage*
Employed	190	59.7
Unemployed	128	40.3
Total	318	100

The above table shows that about sixty per cent of the learners were employed. Only 40 per cent of the first degree learners were unemployed. Thus the first degree programmes of IGNOU are liked more by employed learners. Takwale, 1995 also observed the same phenomenon and reported that 'majority of our students (about 62%) are employed'.

(x) Distribution of Learners by Experience in Distance Learning

Open and distance learning opportunities are available even at the secondary and senior secondary levels through National Open School system at present. In the present study, an attempt was made to know whether the learners had any previous experience in distance learning. The data in this regard are provided in table 4.10.

Table 4.10

Distribution of Learners by Experience in Distance Learning

Category	*Number of Learners*	*Percentage*
Experienced	63	19.8
No Experience	255	80.2
Total	318	100

It is evident from the above table that only about 20 per cent of the learners had experience in learning through distance mode. More than 80 per cent of the learners were freshly enrolled for the first time in learning through distance mode.

(xi) Distribution of Learners by Discontinuity in Studies

Unlike formal system, most of the learners continue their higher education after certain years of gap for various reasons. In the present study, learners were asked to mention the gap (in years) in their studies while getting enrolled to the present course and their previous one. The data in this regard have been presented in table 4.11.

Table 4.11

Distribution of Learners by Discontinuity in Studies

Category	*Number of Learners*	*Percentage*
1-2 years	150	47.2
More than 2 years	168	52.8
Total	318	100

It may be noted from table 4.11 that more than half of the distance learners (52.8%) had a gap of more than 2 years in their studies in reference to the present (BDP) course. However, about 47.2 per cent of the learners had only 1-2 years gap. In some of the earlier studies it was similarly also reported. Sahoo (1985) reported that a large number of learners had 1 to 10 years gap between their last qualifying examination and enrolment in the present course.

Summary

The analysis of the background characteristics shows that majority (67.7%) of the learners were enrolled for the BDP in the year 1991. About 70 per cent learner were male and having age more than 25 years. The percentage of married and unmarried learners were almost equal. About 80 per cent of the learners hailed from urban areas and belonged mostly to non SC/ST and came from arts stream. Further, 52.2 per cent distance learners had no formal qualification (as +2 or equivalent) at the time of getting enrolled for the BDP. About 60 per cent learners were employed. More than 80 per cent had no previous experience in learning through distance mode, and more than fifty per cent had a gap of more than 2 years in their last qualifying examination and enrolment for the present BDP course.

Thus preliminary analysis of background characteristics provides elaborate information about varying characteristics among the first degree level distance learners of the IGNOU. The hypothesis 1 thus appears to have been accepted. These variables may have some influence on the three independent variables selected for the study which will be examined in the following sections.

PART TWO

NATURE OF ACADEMIC SELF-CONCEPT, STUDY HABITS AND ATTITUDE TOWARDS DISTANCE EDUCATION

In this part, the pattern of academic self-concept, study habits and attitude towards distance education for the total sample and the sub-samples formed on the basis of background characteristics of learners have been presented. This part of analysis caters to objective 2 and hypothesis 2 which are stated below.

Objective 2

"To explore the patterns of academic self-concept, study habits and attitude towards distance education among distance learners of Delhi and adjoining areas".

Hypothesis 2

"First degree level distance learners may be found to exhibit varying patterns of academic self-concept, study habits and attitude towards distance education as per their background variables."

In order to test the hypothesis formulated means and SDs were calculated separately for the total sample and sub-samples commensurate with the background variables for three sets of test scores, namely, Academic Self-Concept (ASC) scores, Study Habits (SH) scores and Attitude scores towards Distance Education (ADE).

(i) Nature of ASC, SH and ADE for the Total Sample

Means and SDs were calculated and compared with the norms for knowing the nature of ASC, SH and ADE of 318 sampled distance learners. The data is presented in table 4.12.

Table 4.12

Mean Scores and SDs on ASC, SH and ADE of Total Sample

Variable	*Number of Learners*	*Mean*	*S.D.*
ASC	318	136.96	19.90
SH	318	156.00	21.60
ADE	318	231.50	28.45

Table 4.12 shows that the mean of raw score on the ASC for the total sample was 136.96 with a S.D. of 19.90. On comparing the mean scores with the raw score norms provided in table 3.3 it was noticed that the academic self-concept of first degree level distance learners was above average. In other words, the sampled distance learners appear to possess academic self-concept tilted towards positive side.

Similarly the mean raw score for the Study Habits was found to be 156.0 with a S.D. of 21.60. The mean Study Habits score is indicative of good study habits when compared with the raw score norms provided in table 3.4. Thus it may be concluded that the sampled first degree level distance learners possessed good study habits in general.

The table 4.12 also provides the attitude scores of first degree level distance learners. The mean attitude score was recorded to be 231.50 with a S.D. of 28.45. Its comparison with the raw score norms provided in table 3.6 reveals that the first degree level distance learners' attitude towards distance education was 'above average' and positive. In other words, the sampled distance learners' attitude towards distance education could be assumed to be positive and above average in a global sense.

On the basis of above discussion, it may be concluded that by and large first degree distance learners were found to exhibit above average academic self concept, good study habits and a positive and above average attitude towards distance education.

(ii) Nature of the Distribution for ASC, SH and ADE in Sub-Samples

Sub-samples were formed on the basis of ten background characteristics, *i.e.*, sex, age, marital status, locale, social class, academic stream, educational level, employment status, experience in distance learning and discontinuity in studies. Each of these sub-samples were further classified into dichotomous categories. The means and SDs for ASC, SH and ADE were calculated separately for each of this sub-samples and have been presented in tables 4.13, 4.14 and 4.15 respectively. These are discussed below.

(a) Nature of ASC of Distance Learners for the Sub-Samples

Table 4.13

Mean Scores and SDs on ASC Calculated for Different Sub-Groups

Category	*Group*	*N*	*Mean*	*S.D.*
Sex	Male	215	136.83	20.23
	Female	103	137.24	19.31
Age	Below 25 yrs.	93	138.77	19.15
	25 and above yrs.	225	136.21	20.20
Marital Status	Married	162	139.02	20.12
	Unmarried	156	134.83	19.51
Locale	Urban	249	137.45	20.30
	Rural	69	135.21	18.45
Social Class	SC/ST	61	136.56	20.86
	Non SC/ST	257	137.06	19.71
Academic Stream	B.A.	258	138.21	19.73
	B.Com.	60	131.62	19.93
Educational Level	+2	152	137.58	20.19
	Non+2	166	136.41	19.69
Employment Status	Employed	190	134.91	21.05
	Unemployed	128	140.02	17.72
Experience in Distance Learning	Experienced	63	139.75	22.17
	No Experience	255	136.28	19.29
Discon-tinuity in Studies	1-2 years	150	136.51	21.42
	More than 2 yrs.	168	137.37	18.50

A perusal of table 4.13 reveal that the mean scores on academic self-concept ranged from 131.62 to 140.02. When compared with the norms, the whole range falls in the category of 'above average' (121-160). The range of corresponding SDs was from 17.72 to 22.17. It can, therefore, safely be concluded that the first degree distance learners varying in certain background variables do possess a varying degree of academic self-concept. Yet. not changing the broader category of 'above average' in academic self-concept.

(b) Nature of SH of Distance Learners for the Sub-Samples

Table 4.14

Mean Scores and SDs on SH Calculated for Different Sub-Groups

Category	*Group*	*N*	*Mean*	*S.D.*
Sex	Male	215	156.38	20.86
	Female	103	156.73	23.17
Age	Below 25 yrs.	93	158.47	18.77
	25 and above yrs.	225	155.68	22.65
Marital Status	Married	162	159.51	20.52
	Unmarried	156	153.37	22.30
Locale	Urban	249	156.96	22.11
	Rural	69	154.83	19.69
Social Class	SC/ST	61	161.34	20.80
	Non SC/ST	257	155.34	21.66
Academic Stream	B.A.	258	158.00	21.47
	B.Com.	60	150.02	21.11
Educational Level	+2	152	156.44	21.83
	Non+2	166	156.54	21.45
Employment Status	Employed	190	153.05	22.20
	Unemployed	128	161.61	19.67
Experience in Distance Learning	Experienced	63	161.25	22.52
	No Experience	255	155.32	21.24
Disconti-nuity in Studies	1-2 years	150	156.44	21.84
	More than 2 yrs.	168	156.54	21.44

It may be noticed from table 4.14 that the mean score for study habits ranged from 150.02 to 161.61 for various sub-groups of distance learners. The range of corresponding SDs was from 18.77 to 23.17. This varying pattern of study habits obtaining amongst the distance learners differing in certain background characteristics confirms to the normative range (111-165) which may be considered to represent 'good' study habits. It seems reasonable to believe that the group of distance learners under present study possessed good study habits to a large extent.

(c) Nature of ADE of Distance Learners for the Sub-Samples

Table 4.15

Mean Scores and SDs on ADE calculated for Different Sub-Groups

Category	*Group*	*N*	*Mean*	*S.D.*
Sex	Male	215	231.96	29.83
	Female	103	230.53	25.44
Age	Below 25 yrs.	93	232.58	26.42
	25 and above yrs.	225	231.05	29.29
Marital Status	Married	162	235.01	28.58
	Unmarried	156	227.85	27.94
Locale	Urban	249	231.19	27.90
	Rural	69	232.59	30.54
Social Class	SC/ST	61	230.15	27.76
	Non SC/ST	257	231.82	28.65
Academic Stream	B.A.	258	232.56	28.59
	B.Com.	60	226.93	27.62
Educational Level	+2	152	230.56	29.23
	Non+2	166	232.36	27.78
Employment Status	Employed	190	231.41	29.34
	Unemployed	128	231.63	27.18
Experience in Distance Learning	Experienced	63	230.92	30.73
	No Experience	255	231.64	27.92
Disconti-nuity in Studies	1-2 years	150	229.75	29.20
	More than 2 yrs.	168	233.05	27.76

A close scrutiny of table 4.15 indicates that the mean score on ADE ranged from 226.93 to 235.01 which showed a varying pattern of attitude among the first degree level distance learners. The range of corresponding SDs was from 25.44 to 30.73.

This variation revolves round the category of 'above average' attitude towards distance education which pertains to raw scores from 211 to 280. May be one would be tempted to say that the group under study possessed a positive attitude towards distance education.

Discussion

In the foregoing pages distribution of Academic Self-Concept (ASC), Study Habits (SH) and Attitude towards Distance Education (ADE) for total sample and for sub-samples on the basis of ten background variables have been presented and discussed. It seems worth noting that the variation in sub-groups are seen but do not go far away from the indices obtained for the total sample. It, however, reflects on internal validity of data pertaining to these variables *viz.*, ASC, SH and ADE.

On the basis of the above findings, it may be said that the hypothesis 2 stands accepted. These means and SDs have been put to use for comparison purposes in the analysis which follows in the next section.

Even though there is no research study reported to support the present findings with regard to the academic self-concept and study habits of distance learners, yet, small scale studies showing a positive attitude of students, teachers and of community towards correspondence/ distance education have been found to be available in the literature. The findings of the researchers conducted by Pillai (1980), Khan (1982), Gomati (1982), Sahoo (1985), Sahoo and Bhat (1987), Panda and Chaudhari (1989), Nagpal (1992) show a positive attitude of the learners towards distance education. Thus the findings of the present study seem to confirm the findings of the earlier studies.

PART THREE

STUDY OF ACADEMIC SELF-CONCEPT, STUDY HABITS AND ATTITUDE TOWARDS DISTANCE EDUCATION OF DISTANCE LEARNERS UNDER VARYING BACKGROUNDS

This part of the analysis was accomplished through significance of difference between the mean scores of the sub-groups, formed on the basis of the background variables, on the three test scores namely, academic self-concept, study habits and attitude towards distance education.

In pursuance of the objectives 3 to 5 and hypotheses 3 to 5, a comparative study of the characteristics, namely, academic self-concept, study habits and attitude towards distance education possessed by distance learners, at first degree level, varying in their backgrounds was undertaken.

The details are presented systematically for each of the objective and hypothesis separately in the following paragraphs.

Objective 3

"To study the significance of differences in the academic self-concepts of first degree level distance learners differing in certain background variables".

Hypothesis 3

"First degree level distance learners differ significantly in their academic self-concept according to their varying backgrounds."

The obtained mean scores, SDs and CR values for academic self-concept for pairs under ten background variables were computed and these have been reported in table 4.16.

Table 4.16

Significance of Difference in Academic Self-Concept of First Degree Distance Learners of Varying Backgrounds

Category	*Group*	*N*	*Mean*	*S.D.*	*C.R.*
Sex	Male	215	136.83	20.23	0.17
	Female	103	137.24	19.31	
Age	Below 25 yrs.	93	138.77	19.15	1.04
	25 and above yrs.	225	136.21	20.20	
Marital Status	Married	162	139.02	20.12	1.88
	Unmarried	156	134.83	19.51	
Locale	Urban	249	137.45	20.30	0.83
	Rural	69	135.21	18.45	
Social Class	SC/ST	61	136.56	20.86	0.18
	Non SC/ST	257	137.06	19.71	
Academic Stream	B.A.	258	138.21	19.73	2.33*
	B.Com.	60	131.62	19.93	
Educational Level	+2	152	137.58	20.19	0.53
	Non+2	166	136.41	19.69	
Employment Status	Employed	190	134.91	21.05	2.27*
	Unemployed	128	140.02	17.72	
Experience in Distance Learning	Experienced	63	139.75	22.17	1.24
	No Experience	255	136.28	19.29	
Discontinuity in Studies	1-2 years	150	136.51	21.42	0.39
	More than 2 yrs.	168	137.37	18.50	

* Significant at 0.05 level of confidence.

It may be noted from table 4.16 that the C.R. values for the sub-groups pertaining to academic stream and employment status were obtained to be 2.33 and 2.27 respectively, which were significant at 0.05 level of confidence. The other C.Rs were much below 1.96 and hence may be treated as insignificant. Further, the means of academic self-concept recorded for B.A. and B.Com. distance learners were 138.21 and 131.62 respectively and also the means of academic self-concept for employed and unemployed distance learners were noted to be 134.91 and 140.02 respectively.

It seems fair to assert that the B.A. distance learners and unemployed distance learners possessed significantly higher academic self-concepts as against their B.Com. and employed counterpart distance learners respectively. May be the arts learners and the employed ones have switched over to distance mode of education having faced some of the real life problems which might have induced in them an urge of self-demonstration; and that should have helped them to develop higher academic self-concepts.

Thus the hypothesis 3 was found to hold good only for the background variables of academic stream and employment status of first degree level distance learners.

For the remaining eight background variables, namely, sex, age, marital status, locale, social class, educational level, experience in distance learning and discontinuity in studies, the hypothesis 3 stands rejected. In other words we may say that the first degree level distance learners did not differ significantly in their academic self-concept *vis-a-vis* these eight background variables. The above results have also been depicted through a bar diagram (Fig.2)

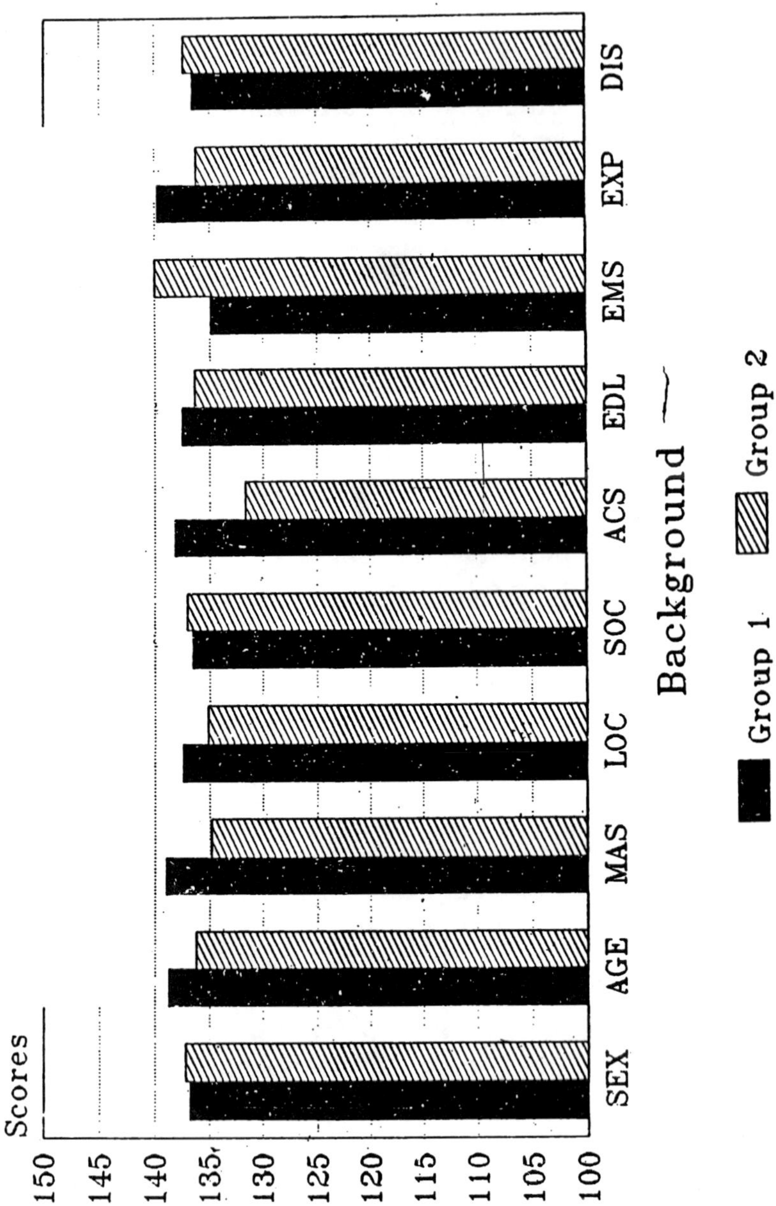

Fig. 2. Bar Diagram showing the ASC of Distance Learners Varying in Different Background Variables

Objective 4

"To examine significance of differences in the study habits of first degree level distance learners *vis-a-vis* their background".

Hypothesis 4

"Significant differences exist in the patterns of study habits of first degree level distance learners on the basis of their background variables."

The statistics pertaining to the testing of hypothesis 4 yielded means, SDs and C.R. values for study habits of first degree level distance learners for the pairs of subjects under each of the ten background variables. The obtained results have been summarized in table 4.17.

An inspection of table 4.17 would reveals that the C.R. values for study habits under five background variables, namely, marital status, social class, experience in distance learning, academic stream and employment status were 2.56, 1.96, 1.96, 2.60 and 3.53 respectively. Out of these C.R. values the first three were significant at 0.05 level of confidence and the last two at 0.01 level of confidence. It may also be noted that relatively higher means were recorded for married (159.51), SC/ST (161.34), experienced ones (161.25), B.A. learners (158.00) and unemployed ones (161.61) as against their respective counterparts.

On the basis of above statistics it may be inferred that significantly better study habits were practised by married learners against unmarried ones, SC/ST learners against non SC/ST learners unemployed learners against employed ones, experience ones against unexperienced ones and B.A. learners as compared to B.Com. learners. This kind of situation leads one to believe that possibly the learners who have realized the importance of further education and are intrinsically motivated to pursue their studies utilizing the opportunity of distance education after long awaiting have acquired some sort of seriousness resulting into better study habits practised by them.

Table 4.17

Significance of Difference in Study Habits of First Degree Distance Learners of Varying Backgrounds

Category	*Group*	*N*	*Mean*	*S.D.*	*C.R.*
Sex	Male	215	156.38	20.86	0.13
	Female	103	156.73	23.17	
Age	Below 25 yrs.	93	158.47	18.77	1.05
	25 and above	225	155.68	22.65	
Marital Status	Married	162	159.51	20.52	2.56*
	Unmarried	156	153.37	22.30	
Locale	Urban	249	156.96	22.11	0.72
	Rural	69	154.83	19.69	
Social Class	SC/ST	61	161.34	20.80	1.96*
	Non SC/ST	257	155.34	21.66	
Academic Stream	B.A.	258	158.00	21.47	2.60**
	B.Com.	60	150.02	21.11	
Educational Level	+2	152	156.44	21.83	0.04
	Non+2	166	156.54	21.45	
Employment Status	Employed	190	153.05	22.20	3.53**
	Unemployed	128	161.61	19.67	
Experience in Distance Learning	Experienced	63	161.25	22.52	1.96*
	No Experience	255	155.32	21.24	
Discontinuity in Studies	1-2 years	150	156.44	21.84	0.04
	More than 2 yrs.	168	156.54	21.44	

** Significant at 0.01 level of confidence.

* Significant at 0.05 level of confidence.

Thus the hypothesis 4 has been accepted for five background variables, namely, marital status, social class, academic stream, employment status and experience in distance learning.

The other background variables of sex, age, locale, education level and discontinuity in studies did not indicate variation in study habits of distance learners at first degree level. In other words the first degree level distance learners varying in sex, age, locale, educational level and discontinuity in studies did not differ significantly with regard to their study habits. The above results have also been depicted through a bar diagram (Fig 3).

Objective 5

"To compare the attitude of first degree level distance learners towards distance education in sub-groups based on the background variables".

Hypothesis 5

"Distance learners at first degree level differ significantly in their attitudes towards distance education with regard to various background variables".

In pursuance of the aforesaid objective and hypothesis, the computations of means, SDs and C.R. values were attempted. The obtained statistics are reported in table 4.18.

A close scrufiny of table 4.18 indicates that the only significant value of C.R. (2.26) is for the background variable of marital status in respect of the attitude towards distance education. The married distance learners had a mean of 235.01 while the mean score for unmarried ones was to the tune of 227.85. The other C.R. values were much short of 1.96. These results indicate that the married students possess significantly higher positive attitude towards distance education as against the unmarried ones.

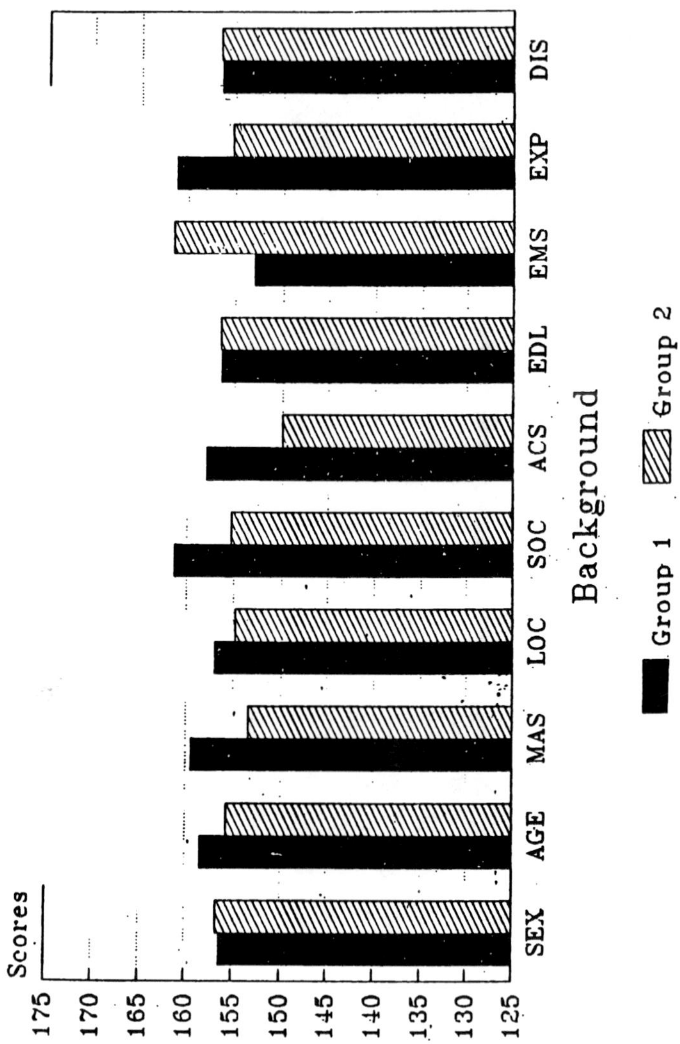

Fig. 3. Bar Diagram showing the Study Habits of Distance Learners Varying in Different Background Variables

Also no significant differences in attitude towards distance education could be noticed among distance learners varying on the remaining nine background variables. *e.g.*, sex, age, locale, social class, academic stream, educational level, employment status, experience in distance learning and discontinuity in studies.

Table 4.18

Significance of Difference in Attitude Towards Distance Education for First Degree Distance Learners of Varying Backgrounds

Category	*Group*	*N*	*Mean*	*S.D.*	*C.R.*
Sex	Male	215	231.96	29.83	0.42
	Female	103	230.53	25.44	
Age	Below 25 yrs.	93	232.58	26.42	0.44
	25 and above yrs.	225	231.05	29.29	
Marital Status	Married	162	235.01	28.58	2.26*
	Unmarried	156	227.85	27.94	
Locale	Urban	249	231.19	27.90	0.36
	Rural	69	232.59	30.54	
Social Class	SC/ST	61	230.15	27.76	0.41
	Non SC/ST	257	231.82	28.65	
Academic Stream	B.A.	258	232.56	28.59	1.38
	B.Com.	60	226.93	27.62	
Educational Level	+2	152	230.56	29.23	0.57
	Non+2	166	232.36	27.78	
Employment Status	Employed	190	231.41	29.34	0.07
	Unemployed	128	231.63	27.18	
Experience in Distance Learning	Experienced	63	230.92	30.73	0.18
	No Experience	255	231.64	27.92	
Discontinuity in Studies	1-2 years	150	229.75	29.20	1.03
	More than 2 yrs.	168	233.05	27.76	

* Significant at 0.05 level of confidence.

Thus the hypothesis 5 was found to hold good only

for the background variable marital status. For the remaining nine background variables, the hypothesis 5 stands rejected. In other words we may say that the first degree level distance learners did not differ significantly in their attitude towards distance education *vis-a-vis* these nine background variables.

However, it may be noted form the findings referred under objective 2 that almost all distance learners were found to possess positive attitudes towards distance education. But the married ones seem to behave still more responsibility while pursuing their studies through distance mode, may be, they develop greater identification with the available access to further education. The above results have also been depicted through a bar diagram (Fig. 4).

Discussion and Interpretation of Results

The preceding paragraphs highlight notable significance of differences in the academic self-concept, study habits and attitude towards distance education in respect of the ten background variables undertaken for the study. In order to have an overview, the results pertaining to objectives 3 to 5 and testing of hypotheses 3 to 5 have been summarized in table 4.19.

It may be noted from table 4.19 that there were no significant differences in the academic self-concept, study habits and attitude towards distance education of first degree distance learners when compared on the basis of sex, age, locale, educational level and discontinuation of studies.

Significant differences exist for five background variables, namely, marital status, social class, academic stream, employment status and experience in distance learning.

Fig.4. Bar Diagram showing the Attitudes of Distance Learners Towards Distance Education

Table 4.19

Significance of Difference in ASC, SH and ADE of First Degree Distance Learners in Respect of Ten Background Variables

Category	*Group*	*ASC*	*SH*	*ADE*
Sex	Male Female	-	-	-
Age	Below 25 25 and above	-	-	-
Marital Status	Married* Unmarried	-	✓	✓
Locale	Urban Rural	-	-	-
Social Class	SC/ST* Non SC/ST	-	✓	-
Academic Stream	B.A.* B.Com.	✓	✓	-
Educational Level	+2 Non+2	-	-	-
Employment Status	Employed Unemployed*	✓	✓	-
Experience in Distance Learning	Experienced* No Experience	-	✓	-
Discontinuity in Studies	1-2 years More than 2 years	-	-	-

Notes : Tick Mark (✓) shows significance of differences.
Asteric (*) mark shows higher mean value.

It may be noted that differences in study habits were observed for all the five variables referred to above. Significance in academic self-concept was noticeable only for the background variable of academic stream and employment status. Significant attitudinal changes was seen only between married and unmarried distance learners.

While examining the background variable's influence on academic self-concept, study habits and attitude towards distance education, it may be observed that social class and experience in distance learning appeared to have significant role in the development of study habits. Significantly better study habits were observable amongst SC/ST learners and those having an experience of learning through distance education. Married distance learners displayed highly significant positive attitude towards distance education as against unmarried ones. Also the influence of academic stream and employment status was visible on academic self-concept and study habits. B.A. learners exceed their B.Com. counterparts in their academic self-concept and study habits. Similarly unemployed learners were much ahead of the employed ones in their academic self-concepts and study habits.

The above findings may be interpreted by stating that the distance education courses are the opportunities which cater to the needs of those who wish to supplement their studies at a later stage. Certain background variables appear to influence the academic self-concept, study habits and attitude towards distance education of distance learners. Particular mention may be made of the choice of stream, employment status, experience in distance learning, social class and marital status. It seems proper to say that the level of earlier deprivation, exposure to real life situation and employment status have an intrinsic effect on the style of thinking and functioning of such learners. This has rightly been reflected in the patterns obtained for unemployed, married, SC/ST learners and those having earlier experience of distance education that they exceed their respective counterparts with regard to study habits and academic self-concept in most of the cases.

PART FOUR

CORRELATES OF ACADEMIC PERFORMANCE OF DISTANCE LEARNERS

This part of analysis has been devoted to the study of relationship between three independent variables, namely, academic self-concept, study habits and attitude towards distance education with academic performance of first degree level distance learners. As such, it meets the requirements of the objectives 6 to 8 and the hypotheses 6 to 8. The objectives and hypotheses are stated below.

Objective 6

"To study the relationship of academic self-concept with academic performance of distance learners at first degree level".

Objective 7

"To investigate into the association of academic performance with study habits practised by distance learners at first degree level".

Objective 8

"To examine the extent of dependence between academic performance and attitude of distance learners towards distance education at first degree level".

Hypothesis 6

"There exists significant positive relationship between academic self-concept and academic performance of distance learners at first degree level".

Hypothesis 7

"There exists significant positive correlation between

study habits and academic performance of distance learners at first degree level".

Hypothesis 8

"Academic performance of first degree level learners is found to show positive and significant correlations with their attitude towards distance education".

In pursuance of the above mentioned objectives and hypotheses, data were gathered only for the distance learners enrolled during 1991 with a view to assessing the impact of three years of study on academic performance of distance learners. Further, the availability of scores on corresponding sets of variables restricted the total number of subjects to 181.

To study the relationship between academic performance and academic self-concept (ASC), study habits (SH) and attitude towards distance education (ADE), Pearsons' Product Moment Correlations were computed. The obtained results have been summarized in table 4.20.

Table 4.20

Coefficients of Correlation between Academic Performance and ASC, SH and ADE

S.No.	*Variable*	*N*	*Coefficients of Correlation with Academic Performance*
1.	ASC	181	0.4714**
2.	SH	181	0.27**
3.	ADE	181	0.24**

** Significant at 0.01 level.

It may be noted from table 4.20 that the obtained coefficients of correlation ranged from 0.24 to 0.4714. All the three correlations were positive and significant. Further, coefficient of correlation between academic self-concept and academic performance was recorded to be 0.4714. It represents moderate positive correlation between the variables. The extent of relationship between academic performance and study habits was obtained to be 0.27. While the interdependence between academic performance and attitude towards distance education was to the tune of 0.24. Both these indices of correlation may be termed as low positive correlation.

The above results indicate that the academic performance depends on patterns of study habits and attitude towards distance education possessed by first degree distance learners. Still more influencing variable seems to be the academic self-concept which has a major share of story to tell. As the coefficients of correlations should be interpreted to show only the inter dependence and not the causation as such, multiple regression analysis has been employed to ascertain the contribution of these predictor variables towards the criterion of academic performance which has been presented in the following part.

On the basis of above discussion, it may be mentioned that the hypotheses stated under 6 to 8 stand accepted. Further, one may like to assert quite safely that the academic performance of distance learners is a function of their academic self-concept, study habits and attitude towards distance education.

Incidentally some of the studies conducted by Marsh (1993), Mc Cabe (1992), Marsh and Parker (1984), Byrne (1984), Radha Rani (1983), Saraswat (1982) and Shavelson and Bolus (1982) reported a positive and high correlation of academic self-concept with academic achievement of formal students.

Researchers focussing specifically on learning styles or study habits and success or failure in distance education have been very limited (Moore, 1985). One of the reasons for this was given by Thompson (1984) that "perhaps some methods of distance education are better suited to some students". However, Thompson (1984) and Moore (1976) suggested a relationship among and between learning styles related variables and completion/satisfaction in distance learning programmes. Similarly the studies conducted by Deb, Madhu (1990), Singh (1984), Shanmuga Sundaram (1983), Tiwari (1982), Jain (1967) and Jamuar (1961) reported a positive and significant correlation between study habits and academic achievement of formal students.

Besides these, a few research studies are available to support the findings pertaining to academic performance and attitude towards distance education. The findings of the present study is also in line with the studies conducted by Sang (1994), Clark (1994), Smith, Dannie (1993) and Gee, Dona (1990). They all reported a positive and significant relationship between academic performance and attitude of distance learners.

PART FIVE

DETERMINANTS OF ACADEMIC PERFORMANCE OF DISTANCE LEARNERS

After having studied relationship of academic self-concept, study habits and attitude towards distance education with academic performance of distance learners, further attempt has been made to predict the academic performance. The linear multiple regression analysis was employed to accomplish the objectives 9, 10 and 11 and test hypotheses 9 and 10. The objectives and hypotheses are stated below.

Objective 9

"To predict academic performance of first degree level distance learners on the basis of their academic self-concept, study habits and attitude towards distance education.

Objective 10

"To study the relative contribution of the predictor variables (Objective 9) towards variance in the criterion *viz.,* academic performance of distance learners at first degree level".

Objective 11

"To draw some significant conclusions with regard to academic performance of first degree level distance learners in the context of the battery of predictor variables".

Hypothesis 9

"A battery comprising of academic self-concept, study habits and attitude towards distance education serves as a good predictor of academic performance of first degree level distance learners".

Hypothesis 10

"Significant amount of variance in academic performance of distance learners at first degree level is attributable to the set of predictor variables; and high, average and low contributions may be made by study habits, attitude towards distance education and academic self-concept respectively."

Prediction of Academic Performance

While applying multiple linear regression analysis,

academic performance was taken as a criterion variable with academic self-concept, study habits and attitude towards distance education as predictor variables. A summary of the multiple regression analysis is presented in table 4.21.

Table 4.21

Prediction of First Degree Distance Learners' Academic Performance (X1) on the Basis of Academic Self-Concept (X2), Study Habits (X3) and Attitude Towards Distance Education (X4)

S. No.	*Predictor Variables*	*Regression Analysis Results for X1*				*% of*
		B	*Beta*	*r*	*Beta x r*	*Contri-bution*
1.	Academic Self-Concept (X2)	0.43007	0.50743	0.4714	0.2392	23.92
2.	Study Habits (X3)	-0.03038	-0.03826	0.27	-0.0103	-1.03
3.	Attitude towards Distance Learning (X4)	-0.0124	-0.02162	0.24	-0.0052	-0.52
	Total R Square				0.2237	22.37

Multiple R = 0.47283
R Square = 0.2237

F = 16.98871*
*Significant at 0.01 Level of Confidence

Adjusted R Square = 0.21041
Standard Error = 14.97691
Constant = —23.65197

Multiple Regression Equation : X1 = 0.43007 X2 — 0.03038 X3 —- 0.0124 X4 —23.65197

Discussion of Results Pertaining to the Prediction of Academic Performance

Scrutiny of table 4.21 reveals that the set of three variables appear to contribute towards the prediction of academic performance of first degree level distance learners. Their combined influence happens to be of the order of 0.47283 as indicated by the multiple correlation. The obtained multiple R represents a moderate positive relationship between academic performance and other three predictor variables, namely, academic self-concept, study habits and academic performance taken together. The relationship was also found to be significant at 0.01 level of confidence. Accordingly the coefficient of determination (R Square) is 0.2237, which suggests that about 22.37 percent of variance in the criterion variable (academic performance) may be accounted for by these 3 variables, namely, academic self-concept, study habits and attitude towards distance education. The rest of the variance (about 77.63%) may be attributed to the variables not included in the prediction battery.

Further, when we try to look into the individual contributions of the variables towards variance in the criterion, we notice that individually academic self-concept appears as the most important predictor with a contribution of 23.92 percent. However, the remaining two variables, namely, study habits and attitude towards distance education signify themselves with negative contributions, although amounting to less than 2 per cent (-1.03 and -0.52 respectively) and act as suppressor variables.

A multiple regression equation has also been developed and reported in table 4.21. This equation may be used to predict the academic performance of first degree learners on the basis of academic self-concept, study habits and attitude towards distance education. The equation appears to suggest that each unit increase in academic self-concept will influence 0.43 unit increment in the criterion variable (academic performance). Contrary to this, unit increase in study habits and attitude towards distance education appear to induce a corresponding decrease of 0.03 and 0.01 units respectively in the criterion variable, the academic performance of first degree distance learners.

On the basis of the discussion presented in the above paragraphs, it seems quite safe to say that the stated hypothesis 9 seems to be holds good. However, the hypothesis 10 does not seem to be tenable as the highest positive contribution was that of academic self-concept while the remaining two variables acted as suppressor variables with negative, although negligible contribution.

On the basis of the above, it may be stated that the academic performance of first degree distance learners may be predicted to some extent on the basis of their academic self-concept, study habits and attitude towards distance education. Emphasis seems to be given to academic self-concept if the academic performance of first degree distance learners is to be enhanced.

Role of Study Habits and Attitude Towards Distance Education as Suppressor Variables

Factors influencing academic performance beyond the present level of prediction would need to be investigated by further research. Role of study habits and attitude towards distance education as suppressor variables is, however, discussed below.

As discussed earlier, in the battery of predictor variables all of them have not been found to contribute positively towards variance in the criterion variable (academic performance). Study habits and attitude towards distance education have been designated as suppressor variables. In order to investigate their role, correlations of these two variables with academic self-concept need to be studied. The data in this regard are presented in table 4.22.

Table 4.22

Coefficients of Correlations of Study Habits and Attitude Towards Distance Education with Academic Self-Concept

Variables	*Number of Learners*	*Coefficient of Correlation*
Academic Self-Concept Vs Study Habits	181	0.6291**
Academic Self-Concept Vs Attitude Towards Distance Education	181	0.5524**

** Significant at 0.01 level of confidence.

A look into the table 4.22 reveals that study habits and attitude towards distance education were found to have coefficients of correlation to the tune of 0.6291 and 0.5524 respectively with academic self-concept. Both these coefficients of correlations represented moderate to high positive relationship with academic self-concept which happens to be significant at 0.01 level of confidence.

The theory of regression analysis suggests that for higher levels of prediction inter correlations among predictor variables should be low as far as possible, which is not in the case of present battery of predictions. This findings suggest that some other variables may be tried to conjuction with academic self-concept in order to arrive at higher levels of prediction of academic performance.

Related Studies : A Discussion

Cookson (1989) reviewed a number of studies and come to a conclusion that "By comparison little research has been devoted to exploring factors that predict the success of distance learners". Furthermore, the research studies that exist have concentrated largely on demographic correlates of students' success.

However, a couple of studies are also being reported in predicting the success of distance learners. To name a few, Greenberg's (1981) study shows that the most significant predictor of course achievement was high school grade point average. Siqueira and Lynch (1986) reported that four out of fifteen variables studied predicted 44 per cent of the variance in successful completion of the course. They are: satisfaction with course, frequency of visits to a local centre, main professional activity while enrolled, and perception of content of instructional material.

Renu's (1990) study reported that five variables, namely, age, previous achievement level, score of total learning strategies, score on overall inter-personal relations and score on overall learners orientation were found to predict the success of the learners' doing B.Ed. through distance mode. Biner P.M. *et. al.* (1995) reported that several personality characteristics were predictive of course performance among the telecourse students.

The results of the present study also add to the existing body of literatures in predicting the success in distance learning. Distance learners' academic self-concept could predict upto 23.92 per cent academic performance, thus showing the contribution of non-cognitive aspects of learner in academic performance.

In the present analysis of multiple regression, the learners' background variables were not employed. As

Wiesner (1983) once noted after reviewing the literature on distance learning 'one very important question still remains to be answered in the field; that is, what are the factors that account for a student's success or failure in distance learning programmes'. The same question may be raised about the subject of the study of the present piece of research. Where in a trial was given to a proposed battery to arrive at dependable conclusions.

PART SIX

SUGGESTED WAYS OF ENHANCING ACADEMIC PERFORMANCE OF DISTANCE LEARNERS

Objective 12

"To suggest on the basis of findings, various ways of enhancing academic performance of distance learners at first degree level".

The correlation analysis presented in part four would lay emphasis on building up a proper academic self-concept, good study habits and a positive and favourable attitude among the distance learners for successful completion of their academic programmes through distance learning.

In order to elaborate further on the issue of suggestions to be incorporated, it may be said that, on the basis of the present study, that somehow necessary attempts should be made to create an environment through the print/non-print media and in personal contacts with distance learners, which may help boost up their academic self-concept besides proving guidance on good study habits, if the performance of distance learners is to be enhanced. On the basis of the above discussion, certain recommendations are presented below.

(i) Enhancing the Academic Self-Concept of Distance Learners

One of the findings of the study is that there exists a

moderate positive and significant correlation between academic performance and academic self-concept of first degree distance learners. This highlights the need of enhancing the academic self-concept of distance learners for better academic performance. Further the prediction analysis shows a variation of 23.92 per cent in academic performance due to the academic self-concept. This highlights the need of building up a positive academic self-concept among the distance learners. The following interventions may be positively contributing in this direction.

Institutional Level Intervention

The clientele for distance learning programmes are normally mature adults. As such, enhancing the academic self-concept of learners have certain limitations. However, at the study centres, the counselling sessions provided by the institution can play a major role in enhancing academic self-concept through developing self-confidence among their learners. In fact, this become an additional work for the respective academic counsellors working in the study centres. The inter-personal communication between the learner and the counsellor must focus on building positive self-concept of learners. The instructional system adopted (both print and other medias) also should provide a healthy environment so that the learner may feel relax in studies.

Learner Initiative

Academic self-confidence may be allowed to boom among distance learners by providing opportunities for more and more participation of learners in various academic activities during contact programmes at the study centres. For this a good rapport between the counsellors and the learners is of paramount importance. The human relationship based on the behaviour and conduct displayed by faculty may have far reaching affect on the tendency of learners for their involvement and participation. If it is encouraged chances of increased academic self-concept are most likely which may in turn be instrumental in enhancing academic performance of learners.

(ii) Improving Study Habits of Distance Learners

The findings of the study also show that there exists a positive and significant relationship between academic performance and study habits of distance learners. In fact, the distance learners have to 'Unlearn' the practises learned in their school in order to become self-learners. On the basis of the present findings the following suggestions are offered to improve the study habits of distance learners.

Institutional Level Intervention

As the learners in distance education system are mostly separated from the parental institution, the learning skills/strategies and study habits of distance learners can only be moulded through proper orientation at the study centres and through the self-instructional materials supplied to them (both print and non-print). The information about how to study, the requirements needed, the ways of attacking the content etc., should be provided with the self-instructional materials. Further, audio and video cassettees may also be developed to provided general orientation about various study skills/ strategies and study habits which a learner might adopt. Again, in the counselling sessions at the study centres, the counsellors must be able to provide the ways and means to go through the instructional materials and developing good study habits.

Learner Initiative

Literatures shows that distance learners employ different

ways of learning through their self-instructional materials. However, a definite study habits will always yields good fruits. The habits like understanding the content, planning the task, working on it with concentration, etc., may act as promoters of good study habits. The distance learners may be impressed upon to choose/develop good and economical study habits which may not have negative influence on physique and mind. For this certain audio-video programmes may be developed to demonstrate various study habits and possible advantages/ disadvantages. The distance learners may be guided to adopt/adapt good practices as per their mental make up and temperament.

In addition to this, it seems worthwhile to make a mention of the study skills provided by Kaye (1988) which the distance learner may follow :

- setting up of personal study objectives;
- development of personal confidence in the ability to study primarily on one's own;
- planning and organising study time and study strategies;
- developing study skills in learning from reading and analysis of self-instructional and other print materials, and, where appropriate, from listening to and viewing broadcasts, using audio and video-tape material, participating in group discussions, and undertaking practical work alone and or in a group situation;
- good communication with the tutor-in writing, by telephone, or at face-to-face meetings. Tutors may play a range of different roles as counsellor, problem solver, provider of feedback, resource persons and assessor.

The above skills are virtually very important and are practically viable to most of the distance learners. Further, the learners may follow the most popular study habits like SQ3R (survey, question, read, recite and review) in their learning.

(iii) Developing a Positive and Favourable Attitude towards Distance Education

The results show that a positive and significant relationship exists between academic performance and attitude of distance learners towards distance education. This lays emphasis on building a positive and favourable attitude among distance learners for their better academic results. Some of the ways are explained below.

Institutional Level Intervention

Satisfaction with the course or programme may lead to have a positive and favourable attitude towards the system. Number of studies enumerate various problems faced by distance learners. However, the present sample of learners had expressed a positive attitude towards distance education in general. Even then, the initiation has come from the side of the institutions to provide adequate and relevant information regarding admission, supplying the instructional materials in time, providing students support system effectively at the study centres, conducting the examination in time, giving effective feedback on assignments, publishing the result in time, etc., etc., and keeping regular touch with the distance learners from time to time. The personal problems (if any) may also be solved at the study centres. The access to the study centres should also be convenient to all learners. Thus once the learner is satisfied with the course/ programme, that may lead to have a positive attitude towards the system.

Learner Initiatives

Optimum utilization of the support system is a major task on the learner's side. Attending more and more counselling sessions, utilising facilities of library and other media available at the study centres, discussion with counsellors and peer learners, timely sending of assignments, appearing in examinations, etc. etc., may help in developing among them positive attitude towards distance education.

The suggestions offered in the foregoing pages may be considered as directions to institutions and learners. However, the distance education institutions should strive to make their programmes more learner friendly and leading to improvement of the academic performance of distance learners.

The main findings of the study, their educational implications and suggestions for further research are summarised in the following chapter.

CHAPTER 5

CONCLUSIONS AND SUGGESTIONS

The previous chapter has been devoted to the analysis and interpretations of data. The analysis have yielded some significant findings pertaining to distance learners' academic performance. The present chapter aims at providing the major findings of the study, educational implications, limitations of findings and suggestions for further research.

Major Findings

The major findings are systematically presented in order of the objectives of the study.

A. Findings Pertaining to the Background Characteristics of Distance Learners

- Majority of the sampled distance learners (67.7%) were enrolled for the Bachelor's Degree Programme (BDP) in the year 1991. The remaining 32.3 per cent learners were enrolled since 1988 and on wards.
- Of the total sample of distance learners, 67:6 per cent were males and the rest of them were females.
- More than 70 per cent of distance learners were in the age group of 25 years and above.
- Marital status-wise, the distance learners were equally divided as married and unmarried ones.

- About eighty percentage of distance learners hailed from urban areas and belonged to non SC/ ST category and pursued B.A. academic stream.
- More than half of the distance learners (52.2%) were not having the basic qualification, *i.e.*, +2 or equivalent certificate at the time of enrolment to the BDP.
- Of the selected distance learners about sixty per cent of them were employed ones.
- Only 19.8 per cent of the learners had an experience of learning through distance mode prior to their present enrolment.
- More than fifty per cent (52.8%) of sampled learners had a gap of more than two years in their studies in reference to the present (BDP) course.

B. Findings Pertaining to the Nature of Distance Learners' Academic Self-Concept, Study Habits and Attitude Towards Distance Education

- The first degree level distance learners were found to possess above average academic self-concept when examined for total sample and the sub-samples based on the background characteristics of learners.
- The first degree level distance learners were found to exhibit good study habits when examined for the total sample and the sub-samples based on the background characteristics of learners.
- The first degree level distance learners displayed above average, positive and favourable attitude towards distance education when examined for total as well as for sub-samples based on the background characteristics of learners.

C. Findings Pertaining to the Significance of Differences Between Means on Distance Learners' Academic Self-Concept, Study Habits and Attitude Towards Distance Education *vis-a-vis* Their Varying Backgrounds

- The first degree level distance learners seemed to differ significantly in their academic self-concept with respect to their academic stream and employment status.
- The B.A. distance learners and unemployed distance learners were found to possess significantly higher academic self-concept as against their counterpart B.Com. and employed distance learners.
- The study habits of first degree level distance learners were found to differ significantly with respect to the five background variables namely: *(i)* marital status, *(ii)* social class, *(iii)* academic stream, *(iv)* employment status and *(v)* experience in distance learning.
- Married distance learners, SC/ST learners, B.A. learners, unemployed distance learners and the learners having experience in distance learning demonstrated better study habits as against their respective counterparts.
- The first degree level distance learners were found to differ significantly in their attitude towards distance education as per their marital status.
- The married distance learners showed significantly higher attitude towards distance education as against their counterpart unmarried distance learners.

D. Findings Pertaining to the Relationship of Distance Learners' Academic Performance with Academic Self-Concept, Study Habits and Attitude Towards Distance Education

- There exist a moderate positive and significant correlation (r=0.4714) between academic performance and academic self-concept of first degree distance learners.

- A low positive but significant relationship (r = 0.27) was noticed to exits between academic performance and study habits of first degree distance learners.

- A low positive and significant relationship (r=0.24) was found to exist between academic performance of first degree distance learners and their attitude towards distance education.

E. Findings Pertaining to the Prediction of Academic Performance of Distance Learners

- A set of three predictor variables *viz.*, academic self-concept, study habits and attitude towards distance education yielded a multiple correlation coefficient of the order of 0.47283 and accounted for about 22.37 per cent of variance in the criterion variable of academic performance of first degree level distance learners.

- Considering the 3 variable battery of predictors, it was found that academic self-concept appeared to be the most important predictor variable with a contribution of 23.92 per cent of variance in the criterion measure academic performance. While the other two (study habits and attitude towards distance education) acted as suppressor variables.

- A prediction equation was developed which is stated below :

  X1 (AP) = 0.43007 X2 (ASC) — 0.03038 X3 (SH) —0.0124 X4 (ADE)—23.65197

  The above equation appears to suggests that for each unit increase in academic self- concept (ASC) first degree distance learners' academic performance (AP) gets increased by 0.43 points. Contrary to this unit increase in study habits (SH) and attitude towards distance education (ADE) appears to induce a corresponding decrease of 0.03 and 0.01 points in the predicted scores.

- On the basis of the present study it may be mentioned that somehow necessary attempts should be made to create an environment through the print/non-print media and in personal contacts with distance learners, which may help boost up their academic self-concept besides providing guidance on good study habits, if the performance of distance learners is to be enhanced. Further, solving the individual problems (if any) and providing maximum facilities of support systems may help developing positive attitude towards distance education among distance learners.

The above findings appear to be significant with a view to streamline this new approach of distance education in the country. Various implications of the study are highlighted in the following paragraphs.

Educational Implications

No research effort can be said to be worthwhile if it does not emanate some of the important educational implications. Research in the area of open and distance education is catching the attention of many researchers. In India, attempts made in this direction are very scanty. However, an attempt has been made in the present piece of research work to investigate the academic self-concept, study habits and attitude towards distance education in relation to academic performance of first degree distance learners. The findings of the study may be utilised in various ways. The findings of the study have certain significant educational implications. These are systematically presented below.

- Analysis of the background characteristics shows a varied nature of distance learners at the first degree level. This may be utilised for future planning of the programmes and need analysis of the learners at the open and distance education institutions/universities.

- Distance education institutions may tailor their self-instructional materials development programme in such a way that it should raise their academic self-concept and inculcate good study habits of learners if quality performance was aimed at.

- Distance education institutions should provide maximum possible facilities to learners in order to develop among them a positive attitude towards distance education in general and their course studies in particular.

- Study centres of the distance education institutions may be equipped with sufficient manpower as well as materials to help the learners to carry out their studies more effectively.

- Counselling sessions should focus on developing

a positive image of the learner in the learning activities.

- Academic Councellor's role needs to be redefined since mere imparting of factual information of the content is not sufficient.
- Monitoring of academic performance has to be done by the distance learning institutions on regular basis inorder to enhance the performance of first degree distance learners.
- Distance learning institutions should not only keep on increasing the enrolment but also keep on their agenda the learning needs of distance learners and address them appropriately.
- Distance learning institutions should devise a mechanism of keeping distance learners highly motivated until the completion of their course.
- Distance learning institutions should make efforts to undertake researches on acceptability of curriculum, changing needs of learners, evaluation procedures, feedback systems and the efficacy of learning materials as their regular future.

Limitations of Findings

The study under reference has yielded several important and interesting findings. An effort was made to make the study as precise and scientific as possible. However, no research study can claim to be prescriptive and may not give final verdict on the phenomenon investigated upon. The findings of the present piece of research do suffer from unavoidable limitations arising out of the constraints of human and material resources and the time at the disposal of the researcher. Besides, the scope of the findings may be limited to the area chosen, tools used, methodology employed, design followed and ultimately the approach utilised for analysis and interpretation of data. These would also be subject to the delimitations envisaged at the planning stage as stated in Chapter 1 as well.

Suggestions for Further Research

No research is the last word in a particular field of study. Every research has its own limitations and also no research can give final verdict about the phenomenon and hence scope for further work is always there. The present piece of research is also no exception to it. However, it is hoped that present piece of research would stimulate some researchers to take-up researches on the issues pertaining to various dimensions of distance education, *e.g.*, efficacy of various strategies on different groups of distance learners, comparative studies, case studies and experimental researches, etc., etc. Having gained some experience through working on the characteristics and performance of distance learners at first degree level, the following suggestions for further researches are offered:

1. This study may be replicated on larger samples and in other Regional Centres of the IGNOU by taking distance learners from different programmes so as to examine the phenomenon in further details.

2. A study may be planned and undertaken to predict distance learners' academic performance by employing a fresh set of variables other than the variables included in the present study.

3. It would be worthwhile to conduct more macro and micro level studies on the nature and characteristics of learners in distance education for effective planning of the programmes of distance education institutions.

4. Studies may be conducted to identify various problems faced by distance learners during their course of study.

5. Impact of various learning skills and learning strategies for distance learners on their academic performance may be studied through experimental research.

6. Case studies may be conducted for acquiring indepth knowledge into the phenomenon of early completion of the course (within the minimum period) and delayed completion of the course by distance learners.

7. A study may be conducted to ascertain the level of satisfaction of distance learners with distance education courses.

8. Studies may be conducted to highlight relationship between distance learners' previous and present academic performance besides exploring reasons for divergent trends.

9. Comparative studies may be taken up to study the influence of institutional inputs on attitudes and performance of distance learners.

10. Experimental studies may be conducted to ascertain the contribution of different media employed in distance education on the academic performance of distance learners.

11. Studies may also be undertaken to assess the extent to which the objectives formulated for various distance education courses/institutions have been realised.

12. Studies may be carried out to investigate cost effectiveness of various distance education courses.

13. Studies may also be planned and executed to explore the influence of motivational factors on accomplishment of distance learners.

The above mentioned suggestions do not represent an exhaustive list of future researches in the area of distance learning. It is, however, an humble attempt to provide stimuli to motivated researchers who should identify research problem of their interest and may derive some basis from the present piece of research and projections made in the preceding paragraphs.

REFERENCES

AIU (1986). National Conference on Distance Education, *University News* (Special Issue), 24 (42), 1-45, New Delhi.

Allport, G.W. (1935). Attitudes. In Murchison, Carl (Ed.), *Handbook of Social Psychology*, Clark University Press, Ch.17.

Anand, S. (1979). *University without Walls*, New Delhi: Vikas Publishing House.

Arora, Asha (1994). Distance Education: A UN Backgrounder, *University News*, 32(21), 1-13.

Artero, Margaret Torres (1989). The use of measures of study skill and attitudes to predict students' achievement in two types of university courses, *Dissertation Abstracts International*, 50(11), 3481#A.

Baath (1982). Distance students' learning—Empirical findings and theoretical deliberation, *Distance Education*, 3(1), 6-27.

Baath, J.A. (1981). On the nature of distance education, *Distance Education*, 2(2), 212-13.

Bachman, J.G. (1970). The impact of family background and intelligence on tenth-grade boys, *Youth in Transition*, Vol.2, Ann Arbor, MI: Survey Research Center, Institute for Social Research.

Barrg, Christine Therese (1991). The relationship among domains of self-concept and academic achievement in learning disabled children, *Dissertation Abstracts International*, 52(3), 842#A.

Basu, Sisir (1994). Distance education and communication channels at Indira Gandhi National Open University, Some perspectives and questions, *Media and Technology for Human Resource Development*, 6(3), 263-271.

Bhattacharya, Sudip (1991). *Open University—Its Scope ana Possibilities: An Analysis of Tagore's Educational Thoughts in Evolving a Conceptual Framework of Open University in India*, Doctoral Dissertation, Visva-Bharati.

Biner, P.M. *et al.* (1995). Personality characteristics differentiating and predicting the achievement of televised course students and traditional course students, *The American Journal of Distance Education*, 9(2), 46-60.

Biswal, B.N. (1979). *A Study of Correspondence Education in Indian Universities*, Doctoral Dissertation, Baroda: M.S. University of Baroda.

Byrne, B.M. (1984). The general/academic self-concept nomological network: A review of construct validation research, *Review of Educational Research*, 54, 427-456.

Byrne, B.M. and Shavelson, R.J. (1986). On the structure of adolescent self-concept, *Journal of Educational Psychology*, 78, 474-481.

Carr, R. and F. Ledwith (1980). Helping disadvantaged students, *Teaching at a Distance*, 18, 77-85.

Calvert, J. (1986). Research in Canadian Distance Education. In J. Mugridge and D. Kaufmann (Eds.), *Distance Education in Canada*, London: Croom Helm.

Cazenave, Anita Washington (1993). The effect of self-concept, school atmosphere, motivation, locus of control and attendance on African-American adolescents' reading achievement, *Dissertation Abstracts International*, 54(2), 470#A.

Chauhan, S.S. and Singh Harbans (1982). An investigation into the study habits of 10 to 12 years of children with regard to their parental profession, *Indian Education Review*, 17(2), 118-22.

Chhabra, N. (1975). A study of certain social psychological variables relating to teachers' morale at secondary and college levels, In Buch, M.B. (Ed.), *Second Survey of Research in Education* (1979). Baroda: Society for Educational Research and Development.

Chilimikolland, M.I. (1987). Action research on study habits and study skills of metallurgy students of Government Polytechnic. In Buch, M.B. (Ed.), *Fourth Survey of Research in Education* (1991), New Delhi: NCERT.

Chisthty, S.B.H. (1992). Achievement motivation, self-concept, personal preferences, students' morale and other ecological correlates in relation to intelligence, socio-economic status and performance of higher secondary tribal students of Rajasthan, *Indian Education Review*, 27(4).

Christain, Z. Maxine (1992). The impact of completion of a basic algebra course on college students' global self-concept and academic self-concept, *Dissertation Abstract International*, 53(8), 2686#A.

Clark, Thomas Allen (1994). Faculty atttiudes toward distance education in U.S. public higher education, *Dissertation Abstracts International*, 54(9), 3293#A.

Clerk, R. Burton and Guy Neave (1992). *The Encyclopedea of Higher Education*: Volume 2. Oxford Pergamon Press.

Coggins, C.C. (1988). Preferred learning styles and their impact on completion of external degree programs, *The Amercian Journal of Distance Education*, 2(1), 25-37.

Coldeway, D.O. (1986). Learner characteristics and success. In J. Mugridge and D. Kaufmann (Eds.), *Distance Education in Canada*, London: Croom Helm, 81-93.

Coldeway, D.O. (1982). A review of recent research on distance learning, In J.S. Danial, M.A. Stroud, and J.R. Thompson (Eds.), *Learning at a Distance: A World Perspective*, Athabasca University/International Council for Correspondence Education.

Cookson, Peter. S. (1989). Research on learners and learning in distance education: A Review. *The Amercian Journal of Distance Education*, 3(2), 22-34.

Das, Mamata (1992). *Approaches to Learning and Academic Performances of Students in Traditional and Open Universities. A Comparative Study*, Doctroal Dissertation. New Delhi: JNU.

Daniel, J.S. (1989). Commonwealth of Learning Opens, *Open Learning*, 4(2), 57-58.

Deb, Madhu *et al.* (1990). Relationship between study habits and achievement of undergraduate Home Science final year students, *Indian Education Review*, 25(3), 71-74.

Dewal, O.S. (1982). *Profile of Registrants—an Enquiry into Variables Relating to Students of Correspondence Institutions of the Secondary Level*, Open School, New Delhi: CBSE.

Dohmen, G. (1977). *Das Fernstudium. Ein neues padagogisches und Entwicklungs feld*, Heidelberg: Quelle and Meyer.

Donga, N.S. (1993). *Factors Relating to Study Skills and Reading Skills of Distance Learners.* Paper presented at International Conference on Educational Technology, New Delhi: AIAET, October 28-30.

Edwards, Allen, L. (1969). *Techniques of Attitude Scale Construction*, Bombay: Vakils, Feffer and Simons Pvt. Ltd.

Ekins, Judith, M. (1993). The development of study processes in distance learning students, *Resources in Education*, 28(8), 14.

Eshel, Yohanan and Kuman, Jenny (1992). Academic self-concept, accuracy of perceived ability and academic attainment, *Psychological Abstracts*, 79(2), 859.

Garrett, H.E. (1966). *Statistics in Psychology and Education*, Bombay: Vakils, Feffer and Simons Ltd.

Garrison, D.R. (1989). *Understanding Distance Education: A Framework for the Future*, London: Routledge.

Gee, Donna Beth Darter (1990). The effects of preferred learning style variables on student motivation, academic achievement and course completion rates in distance education, *Dissertation Abstracts International*, 52(1), 138#A.

Gerald, Steven (1990). Academic self-concept as a predictor of academic success among minority and low socio-economic status students, *Psychological Abstracts*, 78(2), 587.

Giglotti, Card Chafel (1995). The relationship between self-concept of academic ability and academic performance of adult students (28 and older), *Dissertation Abstracts International*, 55(7), 1791#A.

Gilroy, Lindsey (1989). The development and evaluation of

distance learning materials for administrative personnel in a multinational company, *Dissertation Abstracts International,* 50(12), 3822#A.

Gomathi Mani (1982). *A Critical Study of the Participants' Evaluation of Selected Post-Graduate Courses of the Correspondence Education Programme of the Madurai Kamaraj University,* Doctoral Dissertation, Madras: University of Madras.

Goswami, Promod Kumar (1978). A study of self-concept of adolescents and its relationship to scholastic achievement and adjustment. In Buch, M.B. (Ed.), *Third Survey of Research in Education,* (1986), New Delhi: NCERT.

Good, Carter V., Barr, A.S. and Scates, Douglas E. (1941). *The Methodology of Educational Research,* New York: Appleton Century Crofts.

Grudnoski, Anthong Thomas (1992). A descriptive study attitudes and behaviour toward professional continuing education by distance means within 5 professional groups in Marquette country, Michigan, *Dissertation Abstracts International,* 54(1), 60#A.

Greenberg, J.S. (1981). *Expectancy Theory Prediction of Completion Behaviour and Achievement in Correspondence Education,* D.Ed. Dissertation, Pennsylvania State University.

Gupta, L.P. (1978). A study of the personal characteristics and academic achievement of scheduled cast and backward class students of Meerut University. In Buch, M.B. (Ed.), *Third Survey of Research in Education* (1986), New Delhi: NCERT.

Hansford, B.C. and Hattie, J.A. (1982). The relationship between self and achievement/ performance measures, *Review of Educational Research,* 52, 123-142.

Hirunval, A. (1980). A study of pupils' self-concept, academic motivation, classroom climate and academic performance. In Buch, M.B. (Ed.), *Third Survey of Research in Education* (1986), New Delhi: NCERT.

Holmberg, B. (1995). Open Universities: their rationale, characteristics and prospects. In Singh Bakhshish (Ed.), *New Horizons in Distance Education,* New Delhi: Uppal Publishing House.

Holmberg, B. (1990). *Perspectives of Research on Distance Education* (2nd Ed.), Zentrales Institut fur Fernstudienforschung, Hagen.

Holmberg, B. (1989). *Theory and Practice of Distance Education*, London: Routledge and Kegan Paul.

Holmberg, B. (1987). The development of distance education research, *The American Journal of Distance Education*, 1(3), 16-23.

Holmberg, B. (1986). Growth and Structure of distance education, London: Croom Helm.

Holmberg, B. (1977). *Distance Education: A Survey and Bibliography*, London: Kogan Page.

Hom Chaudhuri, S. (1980). An analytical study of correlates of academic performance of college students (Tribal) of Mizoram. In Buch, M.B. (Ed.), *Third Survey of Research in Education* (1986), New Delhi: NCERT.

Honry Ford (1863-1947). 'Anyone who stops learning is old, whether at twenty or eighty. Anyone who keeps learning stays young'. Quoted in Keith Allan Nobal (1995). *The International Education Quotations Encyclopaedia*, Buckingham: Open Univesity Press.

Hotrabhuvananada, Benjaporn (1992). Students' motivational reaction toward self instructional materials of the Thai Open University, *Dissertation Abstracts International*, 53(11), 3787#A.

House, J. Danel (1992). The relationship between academic self-concept, achievement-related expectancies and college attrition, *Psychological Abstracts*, 79(8), 3497.

IGNOU (1995). *IGNOU Prospectus*, New Delhi: Indira Gandhi National Open University.

IGNOU (1992). *Course Materials (I-IV), Master of Arts in Distance Education* (MADE), New Delhi: Indira Gandhi National Open University.

IGNOU (1985). *The Indira Gandhi National Open University Act, 1985*, New Delhi: Indira Gandhi National Open University.

IGNOU (1985). *Indira Gandhi National Open Univesity—Project Report*, New Delhi: Educational Consultants India Ltd.

Indradevi, V. (1985). *Philosophical Analysis of the Concept of Distance Education and its Implications on the Emerging Non-Formal System of Education with Special Reference to Teacher Education*, Doctoral Dissertation, Hyderabad: Osmania University.

Iskandar, Harris (1995). The efficiency of different methods of providing feedback to distance learners in a developing country Universitas Terbuka (U.T.) Indonesia, *Dissertation Abstracts International*, 56(1), 167#A.

Jain, Pushpa Devi (1991). *A Depth Study into the Functioning of Andhra Pradesh Open University*, Doctoral Dissertation, Hyderabad: Osmania University.

Jain, S.K. (1967). Study habits and academic attainment in Uttar Pradesh Colleges. In Buch, M.B. (Ed.), *A Survey of Research in Education (1974)*. Baroda: CASE, M.S. University of Baroda.

Jamuar, K.K. (1961). Investigation of some psychological factors underlying the study habits of college students. In Buch, M.B. (Ed.), *A Survey of Research in Education (1974)*. Baroda: CASE, M.S. University of Baroda.

Jegede, Olugbemiro J. Kirkwood, Jannette (1992). Students' anxiety in learning through distance education, *Resources in Education*, 29(1), 3.

Kaur, Ambika S. (1995). *Customer Expectation and Satisfaction—A Case Study of Distance Education in Management*, Doctoral Dissertation, Patiala: Punjabi University.

Kaye, A.R. (1988). Distance education: The state of the art, *Prospects*, 18(1), 43-54.

Keegan, D. (1986). *Foundations of Distance Education*, London: Croom Helm.

Khan, I. (1982). *Suitability of Teaching English Through Correspondence Courses as Offered by Some Indian Universities at the First Degree Level*, Doctoral Dissertation, Bhubaneswar: Utkal University.

Knowles, M.S. (1978). *The Adult Learner: A Neglected Species* (2nd Ed.), Houston: Gulf.

Knowles, M.S. (1970). *The Modern Practice of Adult Education: Androgogy Versus Pedagogy*, New York: Association Press.

Kulandai Swami and Srinivasan (1994). Facing new challenges through distance education, *Yojana*, 38(1&2), 42-46.

Kulwant Kaur (1974). An investigation of differences existing among over-achieving, normal-achieving and under-achieving, 10th class students in high and higher secondary schools. In Buch, M.B. (Ed.), *Second Survey of Research in Education* (1979), Baroda: Society for Educational Research and Development.

Li, Li-Chun (1995). The effects of effort and worry on distance learning in the National Open University of Taiwan, *Dissertation Abstracts International*, 55(8), 2326#A.

Manav, R.N. (1981). A study of attitudes, self-concepts and values of professional and non-professional college students and relationship of these variables with their achievement. In Buch, M.B. (Ed.), *Third Survey of Research in Education* (1986). New Delhi: NCERT.

Marsh, Herbert W. (1993). Content specificity of relations between academic achievement and academic self-concept, *Psychological Abstracts*, 79(8), 3025. Also in *Journal of Educational Psychology*, 84(1), 35-42.

Marsh, H.W. (1990). Causal ordering of academic self-concept and academic achievement: A multiware, longitudinal panel analysis, *Journal of Educational Psychology*, 82(4); 646-656 and also in *Psychological Abstracts*, 78(5), 1379.

Marsh, H.W., Byrre, B.M. & Shavelson, R.J. (1988). A multifaceted academic self-concept: Its hierarchical structure and its relation to academic achievement, *Journal of Educational Psychology*, 80, 366-380.

Marsh, H.W. and Parter, J.W. (1984). Determinants of student self-concept: Is it better to be a relatively large fish in a small pond even if you don't learn to swim as well? *Journal of Personality and Social Psychology*, 47, 213-231.

Marsh, H.W., Smith, I.D. and Barnes, J. (1985). Multidimensional self-concepts: Relations with sex and academic achievement, *Journal of Educational Psychology*, 77(5), 581-596.

Matt, George, E. *et al.* (1991). High school study habits and early college achievement, *Psychological Abstracts*, 79(6), 2594.

Mc Cabe, Dorothy Louise (1992). The underachieving gifted student: An evaluation of the relationship of learning style and academic self-concept to academic achievement and a case study of one gifted high school students, *Dissertation Abstracts International*, 54(1), 92#A.

Ministry of Education (1963). *Report of the Expert Committee on Correspondence Courses and Evening Colleges*, Delhi: Publication Division.

Ministry of Human Resource Development (1986). *National Policy on Education-1986*, New Delhi: Government of India.

Ministry of Human Resource Development (1986). *National Policy on Education-1986—Programme of Action*, New Delhi: Government of India.

Mishra, K.M. (1991). *Management Patterns, Costs and Academic Effectiveness of Distance Education in Indian Universities*, Doctoral Dissertation. Kurukshetra: Kurukshetra University.

Moore, M.G. (1985). Some observations on current research in distance education, *Epistolodidaktika*, 1, 35-62.

Moore, M.G. (1973). Toward a theory of independent learning and teaching, *Journal of Higher Education*, 44, 661-679.

Mridula (1992). *Economics of Open Learning System: Comparative Cost of Higher Education Through IGNOU*, Doctoral Dissertation, New Delhi: Jawaharlal Nehru University.

Muley, V. *et al.* (1986). *A Review of Correspondence Education*, New Delhi: University Grants Commission.

Murphy, Karen Lee (1990). A qualitative study of attributions in Turkish distance education, *Dissertation Abstracts International*, 51(9), 2998#A.

Nagpal, S. (1992). *Investigation into the Usefulness of Distance Education*, Project Report, Diploma in Distance Education, New Delhi: IGNOU.

NIEPA (1988). Special issue on distance education, *Journal of Educational Planning and Administration*, 2(384), New Delhi: National Institute of Educational Planning and Administration (India).

Omana (1991). *The Study and Problem Solving Habits of College Students*, Doctoral Dissertation, Calicut: University of Calicut.

Owens, Karen B. (1991). An integrative self-enhancement and basic skill program and its impact on students' global self-esteem, academic self-concept, and academic performance, *Dissertation Abstracts international*, 52(4), 1268#A.

Padhi, J.S. (1992). Relationship between classroom environment creativity, academic self-concept and academic achievement, *Journal of Indian Education*, 17(6), 57-60.

Panda, Santosh, K. and S.S. Chaudhari (1989). Attitude, needs and problems of prospective distance teachers, *Media and Technology for Human Resource Development*, 2(1): 45-53.

Panda, S.K., Satyanarayana, P. and Sharma, R.C. (Eds.). (1996). *Open and Distance Education Research: Analysis and Annotation*, Kakatiya University, Indian Distance Education Association.

Pandey, Saroj (1991). Teachers' attitude towards distance education, *Journal of Indian Education*, 16(5).

Pandey, S.K. (1980). *The Economics of Correspondence Education in Indian Universities*, Doctoral Dissertation, Meerut: Meerut University.

Pathman, James Keith (1989). Self and teacher rating of the academic self-concept of black and Mexican American special education students: An exploratory examination, *Dissertation Abstracts International*, 50(11), 3530#A.

Pathni, R.S. (1985). Psycho-social developmental stage (identity vs. role confusion), self evaluation (self-concept) and need (self-analysing) as predictors of academic achievement (actual and perceived). In Buch, M.B. (Ed.), *Fourth Survey of Research in Education* (1991), New Delhi: NCERT.

Patil, G.G. (1984). A differential study of intelligence interest and attitude of the B.Ed. college students as contributory factors towards their achievement in compulsory subjects. In Buch, M.B. (Ed.), *Fourth Survey of Research in Education* (1991), New Delhi: NCERT.

Phythian, T. and M. Clements (1982). Drop-out from third level math course, *Teaching at a Distance*, 21 (Summer), 35-45.

Pillai, J.K. and Mohan, S. (1984). Impact and performance of correspondence education programme of Madurai Kamaraj University. In Buch, M.B. (Ed.) *Fourth Survey of Research in Education* (1991), New Delhi: NCERT.

Pillai, J.K. and S. Mohan (1983). *Impact and Performance of Correspondence Education Programme of M.K. University*, Monograph, Madurai: Department of Education, M.K. University.

Powley, Reger Lynn (1995). The effectiveness of electronic and telecommunications tutoring on distance education students' completion rates, learning outcomes, time to complete, their motivation to participate in future distance education programmes, *Dissertation Abstracts International*, 55(9), 2688#A.

Price, Melissa Lee (1994). Student satisfaction with distance education at the University of South Carolina, *Dissertation Abstracts International*, 54(11), 3964#A.

Priyadarshini, Anita (1994). Support system for a distance learning institute in a developing country, *Innotech Journal*, 18(i), 45-50.

Pugazhenthi, G. (1991). *A Study of Teacher Education Programme through the Correspondence System in Maduai Kamaraj University*, Doctoral Dissertation, Baroda: M.S. University of Baroda. –

Radha Rani (1983). Self-concept and adjustment as factors in academic achievement, *Indian Education Review*, 18(2), 46-59.

Raja Mouli, C. and Rao, P.K. (1993). Study habits of distance learners, *Kakatiya Journal of Distance Education*, 2(2), 39-51.

Ramkumar, Vasantha (1969). Self-concept and achievement in school subjects of prospective university entrants. In Buch, M.B. (Ed.), *A Survey of Research in Education (1974)*, Baroda: CASE, M.S. University of Baroda.

Ram, S. (1984). *An Evaluation of Correspondence Education in Terms of Cost and Academic Performance*, Doctoral Dissertation, Meerut: Meerut University.

Rana, Sudharshana (1992). *A Critical Study of the Distance Education*

Programmes in India in Relation to the Role of IGNOU, Doctoral Dissertation, Shimla: Himachal Pradesh University.

Rana, T. (1986). *A Study of Attitude of Students of M.S. University Towards Distance Education*. Master's Degree Dissertation, Baroda: M.S. University of Baroda.

Rani, B. (1980). Self-concept and other non-cognitive factors affecting the academic achievement of the scheduled caste students in institutions for higher technical education. In Buch, M.B. (Ed.), *Third Survey of Research in Education (1986)*, New Delhi: NCERT.

Rao, D.G. (1965). A study of some factors related to scholastic achievement. In Buch, M.B. (Ed.), *A Survey of Research in Education (1974)*, Baroda: CASE, M.S. University of Baroda.

Rastogi, Anita (1991). Distance Education in the Union Territory of Delhi, *Journal of Indian Education*, 14(6), 52-61.

Rathore, H.C.S. (1991). *A Critical Evaluation of the Systems Adopted for the Management of Teaching and Learning in the Existing Correspondence Institutes in India*, Project Report submitted to NIEPA, New Delhi.

Rathore, H.C.S. (1993). *Management of Distance Education in India*, New Delhi: Ashish Publishing House.

Reddy, R.G. (1992). Distance education, the only alternative, *University News*, 30(22).

Reddy, R.G. (1988). *Open Universities: The Ivory Towers Thrown Open*, New Delhi: Sterling Publishers.

Reddy, V.R. (1994). Learner attitudes and suggestions in distance education. In *Distance Education: An Interface*, Hyderabad: BRAOU.

Rekkedal, T. (1983). Enhancing student progress in Norway, *Teaching at a Distance*, 23 (Summer), 19-24.

Renu, Arun (1990). *A Study of Success in Distance Learning System in Relation to Some Key Learned and Institutional Variables*, Doctoral Dissertation, Kurukshetra: Kurukshetra University.

Riddle, Joy Frances (1995). Factors which contribute to grade achievement and course satisfaction of distance education students, *Dissertation Abstracts International*, 55(9), 2743#A.

Roberts, Lowell Harlbut (1991). Educational goals and self-concepts of distance learners at empire college, *Dissertation Abstracts International*, 51(11), 3602#A.

Rumble, G. (1989). On defining distance education, *The American Journal of Distance Education*, 3(2), 8-21.

Saga, Hiroo (1993). Students and tutors perceptions of learning at Allama Iqbal Open Univesity, *Resources in Education*, 28(10), 101.

Sahoo, P.K. (1994). *Open Learning System*, New Delhi: Uppal Publishing House.

Sahoo, P.K. (1985). *A Study of the Correspondence Education in an Indian University*, Doctoral Dissertation, Baroda: M.S. University of Baroda.

Sahoo, P.K. and Bhat, V.D. (1987). Students attitude towards correspondence system of education, *Journal of Indian Education*, 13(2), 28-33.

Saini, R.K. (1979). *An Evaluative Study of the Correspondence Course Run by the Punjab Agricultural University: Ludhiana for farm - Women*, Doctoral Dissertation, Ludhiana: Punjab Agricultural University.

Sang-Jan, Pattama (1994). Learning strategies and attitudes of adults in a distance basic education programme in Thailand and their relationship to the students' academic achievement, *Dissertation Abstracts International*, 54(9), 3409#A.

Saraswat, R.K. (1982). A study of self concept in relation to adjustment, values, academic achievement, Socio-economic status and sex of high school students of Delhi. In Buch, M.B. (Ed.), *Fourth Survey of Research in Education* (1991), New Delhi: NCERT.

Saxena, S.K. (1981). Self-concept, study habit and school attitude as correlates of socio-economic status and cultural setting in different divisioners and failures of high school students of Kanpur district. In Buch, M.B. (Ed.), *Third Survey of Research in Education* (1986), New Delhi: NCERT.

Sesharatnam, C. (1994). *Multi-media Instructional System in Distance Education: A Case Study of Dr. B.R. Ambedkar Open University,* Doctoral Dissertation, Hyderabad: Osmania University.

Shanmuga Sundaram, R. (1983). An Investigation into factors related to academic achievement among undergraduate students under semester system. In Buch, M.B. (Ed.), *Fourth Survey of Research in Education* (1991), New Delhi: NCERT.

Shavelson, R.J. and Bolus, R. (1982). Self-concept: The interplay of theory and methods, *Journal of Educational Psychology,* 74, 3-17.

Shavelson, R.J., Hubner, J.J. and Stanton, C.G.(1976). Self-concept: validation of construct interpretations, *Review of Educational Research*, 46(3), 407-441.

Shejwal, B.R. (1980). Investigation into study habits of college students. In Buch, M.B. (Ed.), *Third Survey of Research in Education* (1986), New Delhi: NCERT.

Singh, A.D. (1983). A comparative study of high and low academic achievers in self-concept formation. In Buch, M.B. (Ed.), *Fourth Survey of Research in Education* (1991), New Delhi: NCERT.

Singh, B. (1986). A study of some possible contributing factors to high and low achievement in Mathematics of the high school students of Orissa. In Buch, M.B. (Ed.), *Fourth Survey of Research in Education* (1991), New Delhi: NCERT.

Singh, Bakshish, *et al.* (1993). *Correspondence or Distance Education in India: An indepth Study Covering the Year 1989-90,* Research Report, New Delhi: IGNOU.

Singh, H. (1984). A survey of the study habits of high, middle and low achiever adolescens in relation to their sex, intelligence and socio-economic status. In Buch, M.B. (Ed.), *Fourth Survey of Research in Education* (1991), New Delhi: NCERT.

Siqueira de Freitas, K. and Lynch, P. (1986). Factors affecting student success at the National Open University, Venezuela, *Distance Education*, 7(2), 191-200.

Smith, Dennie L. Mc Nelis Mary, J. (1993). Distance education: Graduate student attitudes and academic performance, *Resources in Education*, 29(1), 81.

Snodgrass, Rosemary Black (1989). A study of locus of control, achievement motivation and knowledge and use of study skills as factors influencing academic performance in academically talented college students. *Dissertation Abstracts International*, 50(12), 3856#A.

Sparkers, J. (1983). The problem of creating a discipline of distance education, *Distance Education*, 4(2), 197-205.

Srivastava, Manjulika (1995). *Effectiveness of Distance Education: A Case Study of Karnataka State*, Doctoral Dissertation, New Delhi: Jamia Millia Islamia.

Suciati (1990). The effect of motivation on academic achievement in a distance education setting: An examination of latent variables in an Indonesian case, *Dissertation Abstracts International*, 52(4), 1181#A.

Sunanda, G. (1980). The effects of counselling on the study habits and achievement of teacher trainees. In Buch, M.B. (Ed.), *Third Survey of Research in Education* (1986), New Delhi: NCERT.

Sween (1984). Academic achievement of high school students in relation to instructional design, intelligence, self-concept and n-achievement. In Buch, M.B. (Ed.), *Fourth Survey of Research in Education* (1991), New Delhi: NCERT.

Swennumson, Sharon Terpstra (1992). The effect of the SQ3R study method on reading comprehension of non-traditional college students, *Dissertation Abstract International*, 53(7), 2209#A.

Sylves, Ann Frances (1993). Experimental exploration of causal direction between self-concept and achievement, *Dissertation Abstracts International*, 54(2), 468#A.

Takwale, Ram. G. (1995). Sixth Convocation Report of IGNOU, *University News*, 32(25), 18-20.

Terry Evans and Dargl Nation (1993). *Reforming Open and Distance Education: Critical Reflection from Practice*, Kogan Page.

Thompson, D.G. (1984). *Designing for Diversity: The Interaction Between Cognitive Style of Field Dependence/Independence and the Provision or Absence of Systematic Telephone Tutoring upon Persistence and Course Evaluation Scores of Students Enrolled in Correspondence Study*, Doctoral Dissertation, University of Wisconsin - Madison.

Tiwari, G.N. (1982). Study habits and scholastic performance at three levels of education. In Buch, M.B. (Ed.), *Fourth Survey of Research in Education* (1991), New Delhi: NCERT.

Trivedi, R.S. and Patel, B.V. (1973). Comparative study of the performance and study habits of students reading in B.A. (English) and B.A. (Non-English) course of S.P. University. In Buch, M.B. (Ed.), *Second Survey of Research in Education* (1979), Baroda: Society for Educational Research and Development.

University News (1995). *The Mainstay of Tertiary Education: A Report of the Sixth Convocation of INGOU*, New Delhi, 32(25), 16-18.

University Grants Commission (1981). UGC guidelines for correspondence courses, *University News*, 19(21).

Upreti, D.C. (1988). *Impact of Teacher Training Through Correspondence Course (B.Ed., SCCC) on Upward Occupational Mobility of the Elementary Teacher in Western Region*, Bhopal: Regional College of Education.

Venkataiah, N. (1989). Preparation of course material for distance education: Course team approach, *Indian Education Review*, 24(4), 39-46.

Vijayalakshmi Pandit, P. (1994). *Role of Distance Education in Empowerment of Women - A Case Study of Dr. B.R. Ambedkar Open University*, Doctoral Dissertation, Hyderabad: Osmania University.

Wedemayer, C.A. (1977). Independent Study. In A.S. Knowles (Ed.), *The International Encyclopedia of Higher Education*, Boston: CIHED.

Westfall, Beth Davies (1991). The development and implementation of an academic and non-academic support system for distance learners at Brandon University, *Dissertation Abstracts International*, 52(6), 1990#A.

Whlhite, Stephen C. (1992). Self-concept of academic ability, academic aptitude, and study activities as predictors of college course achievement, Resources in Education, 28(2), 157.

Wiesner, P. (1983). Some Observations on telecourse research and practice, *Adult Education Quarterly*, 33(4), 215-21.

Willen, B. (1981). Distance Education at Swedish Universities: An evaluation of the experimental programme and a follow up study, *Uppalsa Studies in Education*, 16, 301.

Woodley, A. and M. Parlett (1983). Student dropout, *Teaching at a Distance*, 24, 2-23.

Yeh, Hsiang-Yeng (1991). The relationship of academic achievement to the variables of achievement motivation, study habits, intellectual development and junior college students in the Republic of China, *Dissertation Abstracts International*, 52(3), 859#A.

Appendix

ACADEMIC SELF-CONCEPT, STUDY HABITS AND ATTITUDE OF DISTANCE LEARNERS

GENERAL INSTRUCTIONS:

1. Give your responses by ticking (√) the appropriate answers in the following proforma.
2. Do not leave any statement without answering.
3. Do not write any thing on the box given in the left side.
4. Your responses will be kept strictly confidential and used for research purpose only.

BACKGROUND INFORMATION

Roll No. : ☐☐☐☐☐☐☐☐☐ Year of Admission : ☐☐☐☐

Name : ______________________

☐ Sex	: 1. Male	2. Female	☐ Age	: 1. Below 25	2. 25 & above
☐ Marital Status	: 1. Married	2. Unmarried	☐ Local	: 1. Urban	2. Rural
☐ Category	: 1. SC/ST	2. Others	☐ Course	: 1. B.A. 2. B.Sc	3. B.Com
☐ Academic Qualification	: 1. +2 Pass	2. Non+2	☐ Whether Employed	: 1. Yes	2. No
☐ Discontinuity In Studies		1. 1-2 years	2. More than 2 years		
☐ Previous Experience In Distance Learning	: 1. Yes	2. No			

1. Academic Self Concept Scale for Distance Learners

Here are some statements relating to your academic and educational aspects. Each statement is associated with five possibilities of your responses *viz.* **Strongly Agree (SA), Agree (A), Undecided (UD), Disagree (D) and Strongly Disagree (SD)**. Please go through each statement carefully and give your response by ticking on(√) any one of the five responses given.

☐ The course I joined is in accordance with my capabilities.	SA	A	UD	D	SD
☐ My friends always call me a duffer (budhu).	SA	A	UD	D	SD
☐ I forget the things immediately after which I have learnt it.	SA	A	UD	D	SD
☐ I possess ability to succeed in higher education.	SA	A	UD	D	SD
☐ I am not able to study with full concentration yet.	SA	A	UD	D	SD
☐ I have no interest in studying certain subjects.	SA	A	UD	D	SD
☐ I work very hard in my studies.	SA	A	UD	D	SD
☐ From my school days itself I have been very weak in studies.	SA	A	UD	D	SD
☐ I feel irritating when I open my books for studying.	SA	A	UD	D	SD
☐ I cannot progress in learning as I don not possess the pre-requistites.	SA	A	UD	D	SD
☐ I do not want to hide my academic weakness to friends and teachers.	SA	A	UD	D	SD
☐ I always plan about my studies.	SA	A	UD	D	SD
☐ I get less time for studies.	SA	A	UD	D	SD
☐ I am not able to do my homework and assignments in time.	SA	A	UD	D	SD
☐ I spend a lot of time in library for study purpose.	SA	A	UD	D	SD
☐ I feel difficulty in sparing time for studies at home.	SA	A	UD	D	SD
☐ I am over-burdened with my academic work.	SA	A	UD	D	SD
☐ I do my work in advance.	SA	A	UD	D	SD
☐ I have not yet learned the good technique of study.	SA	A	UD	D	SD
☐ I appear in the examination without sufficient preparation.	SA	A	UD	D	SD
☐ I think I am not getting proper guidance in my studies.	SA	A	UD	D	SD

☐	I home I shall complete the course within the minimum possible period.	SA	A	UD	D	SD
☐	I may not be able to complete my course successfully.	SA	A	UD	D	SD
☐	I am very optimistic towards my studies.	SA	A	UD	D	SD
☐	I think I can pass the course easily.	SA	A	UD	D	SD
☐	After completing the course, I have very bright prospects.	SA	A	UD	D	SD
☐	I spend much of the time worrying over the future.	SA	A	UD	D	SD
☐	I am confident of getting good grade in my examination.	SA	A	UD	D	SD
☐	I am not afraid of competition.	SA	A	UD	D	SD
☐	I am very much worried about the examination.	SA	A	UD	D	SD
☐	Self-study method is very suitable to me.	SA	A	UD	D	SD
☐	Teachers, teaching during contact programmes do not impress me.	SA	A	UD	D	SD
☐	I have to leave my studies and start a vocation because of my family conditions.	SA	A	UD	D	SD
☐	I give more importance to my studies than any other work.	SA	A	UD	D	SD
☐	I think I could study better in regular class.	SA	A	UD	D	SD
☐	I have joined the course just for getting one more degree.	SA	A	UD	D	SD
☐	I think discontinuity in my study is making a lot of problems to study now.	SA	A	UD	D	SD
☐	I feel very loneliness in my studies through distance mode.	SA	A	UD	D	SD
☐	I think distance mode of education is not suitable for me.	SA	A	UD	D	SD
☐	I am always delayed in sending my assignments.	SA	A	UD	D	SD

2. Study Habit Inventory

Here are some statements regarding your study related activities. Each statement is associated with four possibilities of your responses *viz.* **Never (N), Sometimes (ST), Mostly (MS) and Always (AL)**. Please go through each statement carefully and give your response by ticking (√) on any one of the four responses given.

☐	I learn with proper understanding of definitions, formulae, etc. used in the subject matter.	N	ST	MS	AL

☐ I use the knowledge of one subject in other areas.	N	ST	MS	AL
☐ I understand the main points of a chapter during its first reading.	N	ST	MS	AL
☐ While writing the answers in the examination, I pay special attention to principles of language and spelling.	N	ST	MS	AL
☐ In my studies, I devote comparatively more time to one or two subjects than other subjects.	N	ST	MS	AL
☐ After reading the subject matter I write down its main points/summary.	N	ST	MS	AL
☐ I remain puzzeled at what should I read.	N	ST	MS	AL
☐ Before starting studies, I decade in advance as to how much I would cover.	N	ST	MS	AL
☐ I plan the answers to the examination questions sequentially according to their importance.	N	ST	MS	AL
☐ I study daily at the definite place and time.	N	ST	MS	AL
☐ Before attempting to answer the question, I collect the maximum possible related subject matter.	N	ST	MS	AL
☐ In the examination hall I take precaution to save some time in order to go through the answers once again.	N	ST	MS	AL
☐ I generally study unsystematically and irregularly.	N	ST	MS	AL
☐ After diagnosing my study related difficulties, I take steps to remove them.	N	ST	MS	AL
☐ Before writing answers in examination, I prepare an outline of it.	N	ST	MS	AL
☐ Inspite of feeling bored in work related to studies I do not leave it in between.	N	ST	MS	AL
☐ I continue my studies uniformly in every month through out the year.	N	ST	MS	AL
☐ Whenever I appear in the examinations without receiving prior information then either I fail or get less marks.	N	ST	MS	AL
☐ I continue studying until I complete the work decided for the day.	N	ST	MS	AL
☐ I keep in touch with the work of next class during summer vacations.	N	ST	MS	AL
☐ I do most of my studies with the help of keys, guides, helpbooks, etc.	N	ST	MS	AL

☐	I wake up early morning and study.	N	ST	MS	AL
☐	My daily study time is so short that I find myself unable to concentrate on my studies.	N	ST	MS	AL
☐	I burn mid night oil during examination days.	N	ST	MS	AL
☐	I devote the maximum possible time in my studies.	N	ST	MS	AL
☐	I keep my studies complete through regular studies.	N	ST	MS	AL
☐	I carefully take down notes partaining to each subject.	N	ST	MS	AL
☐	While studying I note down such subject matter which prove useful afterwords.	N	ST	MS	AL
☐	While reading I take notes in such a manner that the important points are highlighted distinctly.	N	ST	MS	AL
☐	I prepare notes from the books in my own words.	N	ST	MS	AL
☐	I think useless things while reading.	N	ST	MS	AL
☐	I am unable to study competently because I feel tired as I started studying.	N	ST	MS	AL
☐	I remain worried while studying.	N	ST	MS	AL
☐	Generally, I fully get involved in studies.	N	ST	MS	AL
☐	I concentrate on study for a short period only.	N	ST	MS	AL
☐	My attention towards studies is diverted due to activities related to picnic, elections and planning for the future.	N	ST	MS	AL
☐	I fail to understand the subject matter if I continue studying for a long time.	N	ST	MS	AL
☐	I feel disturbed in my studies because of the ideas of seeking sympathy and support from teachers.	N	ST	MS	AL
☐	The change of climate hinders my daily programme of study.	N	ST	MS	AL
☐	The worry regarding failure in the examination is an obstacle in my studies.	N	ST	MS	AL
☐	I leave the difficult task to be completed in future.	N	ST	MS	AL
☐	I carelessly complete the difficult chapters as soon as possible.	N	ST	MS	AL
☐	I sort out the probable questions of chapter and write down their answers to unable me to respond suitably whenever needed.	N	ST	MS	AL

☐ I do not show enthusiasm even in reading interesting subjects.	N	ST	MS	AL
☐ I study each subject of the syllabus with full involvement whether or not it is interesting.	N	ST	MS	AL
☐ I leave the difficult chapter with irritation and dissatisfaction.	N	ST	MS	AL
☐ While reading long chapters, I frequently repeat in mind the main points and principles.	N	ST	MS	AL
☐ I revise most of the subject matter related to examination during the previous night of the examination day.	N	ST	MS	AL
☐ I consult the dictionary to find out the meanings of newly used words in the chapter.	N	ST	MS	AL
☐ I note down the new words in order to improve my vocabulary.	N	ST	MS	AL
☐ After reading several pages of the book I will not be able to give immediately an explanation of the subject matter.	N	ST	MS	AL
☐ I memorise the chapter which I do not understand.	N	ST	MS	AL
☐ I take advise of my counsellors about study related problems.	N	ST	MS	AL
☐ I take help of my colleagues whenever I do not understand the actual meaning of the question.	N	ST	MS	AL
☐ I do not receive much help from anybody in my studies.	N	ST	MS	AL

3. **Attitude Scale Towards Distance Education**

Here are some statements pertaining to various aspects of distance education. Each statement is associated with five possibilities of your response *viz.* **Strongly Agree (SA), Agree (A), Undecided (UD), Disagree (D), and Strongly Disagree (SD).** Please go through each statement carefully and give your response by ticking (√) on any one of the five responses given.

☐ Distance education helps in controlling undue rush to the conventional colleges/institutions.	SA	A	UD	D	SD
☐ Distance education is less expensive mode than that of formal education.	SA	A	UD	D	SD

☐ The degree/diplomas obtained through distance education are not valued as those through the formal system.	SA	A	UD	D	SD
☐ Distance education has a bright future in India.	SA	A	UD	D	SD
☐ Generally weak students join courses through distance education.	SA	A	UD	D	SD
☐ Distance education is more useful for working people to upgrade their qualifications.	SA	A	UD	D	SD
☐ Quality of learning through distance education is not at all inferior to the learning through regular classroom.	SA	A	UD	D	SD
☐ Distance mode of education is not suitable for professional/technical education.	SA	A	UD	D	SD
☐ Most of the distance learners are careless in their studies.	SA	A	UD	D	SD
☐ Distance education provides opportunities to the persons neglected so far, for higher education.	SA	A	UD	D	SD
☐ In distance education mode, information regarding starting of course is not made available in advance.	SA	A	UD	D	SD
☐ Admissions to distance education courses are free from regional/state biases.	SA	A	UD	D	SD
☐ Out of those admitted to distance education courses, a very limited number of learners complete the course.	SA	A	UD	D	SD
☐ Previous achievements how so ever low, do not come into the way of pursuing the studies through distance mode.	SA	A	UD	D	SD
☐ Due to lack of sophistication of admission procedure in distance education, many students pursue two courses at a time.	SA	A	UD	D	SD
☐ The self-instructional materials provided in distance mode are very easy to understand.	SA	A	UD	D	SD
☐ Generally the study materials are not made available in time to the distance learners.	SA	A	UD	D	SD
☐ The activities included in the self-instructional materials promote habit of independent study.	SA	A	UD	D	SD

☐	The course materials provided are too bulky and burdensome.	SA	A	UD	D	SD
☐	The language used in the self-instructional materials is quite comprehensible.	SA	A	UD	D	SD
	The self-instructional materials are effective enough to replace the teacher.	SA	A	UD	D	SD
☐	The self-instructional materials are not-adequate enough to prepare for examination.	SA	A	UD	D	SD
☐	The supplementary materials supplied do not encourage further reading.	SA	A	UD	D	SD
☐	The self-instructional materials supplied are generally stereo typed and out dated.	SA	A	UD	D	SD
☐	Self-instructional materials of distance education do really help in self-learning.	SA	A	UD	D	SD
☐	Generally the audio/video materials used in distance education are of very poor quality.	SA	A	UD	D	SD
☐	The timing of the Television broadcasts is generally suitable to the distance learners.	SA	A	UD	D	SD
☐	Normally Television broadcast is not watched by most of the distance learners.	SA	A	UD	D	SD
☐	The audio/video materials and Television broadcasting helps in clarifying some of the concepts in the print material.	SA	A	UD	D	SD
☐	Generally schedules of Television broadcasting are not make available in time to the distance learners.	SA	A	UD	D	SD
☐	It is the multi-media instruction which has a far reaching effect on the learning of distance learners.	SA	A	UD	D	SD
☐	Generally various media employed in distance education lack coordination.	SA	A	UD	D	SD
☐	Unless the frequency of Television broadcasting is increased distance learning may not be effective.	SA	A	UD	D	SD
☐	The facility of issuance of audio-video cassettes is not properly extended to learners.	SA	A	UD	D	SD
☐	There are too many assignments required to be sent by the learners.	SA	A	UD	D	SD

☐ The compulsion of sending required number of assignments helps the learner to go through the study materials carefully.	SA	A	UD	D	SD
☐ There is not proper time gap between two assignments to be sent.	SA	A	UD	D	SD
☐ In general, grading of assignments is not done properly.	SA	A	UD	D	SD
☐ Generally the assignments are not returned back before the turn end examination.	SA	A	UD	D	SD
☐ Responding to the assignments is a rewarding experience.	SA	A	UD	D	SD
☐ The remarks made by the counsellor on the assignments are not educative.	SA	A	UD	D	SD
☐ Sincere attempting on assignments helps in getting good grade in the final examination.	SA	A	UD	D	SD
☐ Writing assignment is really a very boring task.	SA	A	UD	D	SD
☐ The system of sending required number of assignments as a compulsory for appearing examination should be abolished.	SA	A	UD	D	SD
☐ The counselling sessions are generally hopeless.	SA	A	UD	D	SD
☐ Interaction with the counsellors help in developing new insights	SA	A	UD	D	SD
☐ Generally counselling sessions are starved of necessary facilities and equipments.	SA	A	UD	D	SD
☐ Counselling sessions help to remove isolation in studies.	SA	A	UD	D	SD
☐ Generally the dates of organising counselling sessions are not communicated in advance.	SA	A	UD	D	SD
☐ The number of counselling sessions are too less to make any impact.	SA	A	UD	D	SD
☐ Two-way communication between the counsellor and the learner helps to arouse interest in studies.	SA	A	UD	D	SD
☐ Generally counsellors are in-experienced persons in the field of distance teaching.	SA	A	UD	D	SD
☐ For distance learners attending counselling classes should be made optional.	SA	A	UD	D	SD
☐ Generally the library facilities at the study centres are adequate.	SA	A	UD	D	SD

☐ Generally the study centres are located at inconvenient places.	SA	A	UD	D	SD
☐ Postponement of counselling classes is a regular feature in the study centres.	SA	A	UD	D	SD
☐ Study centres are not well equipped to provide adequate information regarding admission to various courses.	SA	A	UD	D	SD
☐ The staffs of study centre generally cooperate with the students.	SA	A	UD	D	SD
☐ Generally the study centres fail to provide an institutional climate for distance learners.	SA	A	UD	D	SD
☐ Generally study centres lack in physical facilities.	SA	A	UD	D	SD
☐ Generally the study centres are the means of arranging for gossiping.	SA	A	UD	D	SD
☐ Generally the scheme of examination is realistically planned.	SA	A	UD	D	SD
☐ Normally distance learners appear for examinations without much of the preparations.	SA	A	UD	D	SD
☐ Generally the examination questions in distance education do not test proper understanding of the content.	SA	A	UD	D	SD
☐ Grades provided in distance education reflect genuine measure of achievement.	SA	A	UD	D	SD
☐ Distance mode examinations do not promote competitive spirit for better learning.	SA	A	UD	D	SD
☐ There are too many formalities to be completed before the examination are held.	SA	A	UD	D	SD
☐ Un realistic allotment of the examination centres for distance education cause great inconvenience.	SA	A	UD	D	SD
☐ It is not feasible to attempt the whole question paper in the given time limit.	SA	A	UD	D	SD
☐ Delivery of intimation cards at the eleventh hour has a negative effect on achievement of learners.	SA	A	UD	D	SD

INDEX